Dying in the Sun

Dying in the Sun

DONN PEARCE

Charterhouse New York

DYING IN THE SUN

COPYRIGHT © *1974* BY *Donn Pearce*

Portions of this book have appeared in different
form in *Esquire, Miami Herald, Playboy, Oui, Capitalist Reporter*

LIBRARY OF CONGRESS CATALOG CARD NUMBER: 79–89338

ISBN–88327–032–3

MANUFACTURED IN THE UNITED STATES OF AMERICA

Dying in the Sun

✳   ✳   ✳

He was twenty. He was healthy, his clothes good, his car new. He had grown up in St. Petersburg, had gone to high school with the girl sitting there beside him on the front seat. In two weeks they were going to be married. He drove past the park and the sidewalk benches and past the green wicker rocking chairs on the wooden porches and the wheelchair ramps built against the curbstones at every corner. As he drove he kept looking up into the rearview mirror at the other St. Pete girl sitting in the back seat.

And then the three of them were remembering those downtown characters they all knew when they were school kids, giggling as they reminded one another of the old spastic called Screwy Louie. Creeping Jesus had a house on the south side, his entire living room covered with pictures of Christ. There was the old lady called Granny Hart whose house was found full of rolls of black crepe when she died. All the kids just knew that somewhere hidden away were boxes of diamonds that her husband had left her from his mine in South Africa. And then there was the old lady who always wore a complete outfit of navy blue. She was very thin. Her hair was white and she wore large dark sunglasses. Every day she walked over the exact route the bus had taken that time long ago when it ran over and killed her husband.

The car started and stopped and turned. The driver kept looking up into the mirror as he talked, as he smiled, as he quoted Johnny Carson saying that St. Petersburg was a city of the newly wed and the nearly dead. And then he told the story of the heart-attack contest. A number of students at Florida Presbyterian College got together a pool. Everybody put in ten dollars and swore an oath of honesty. The one who personally witnessed the greatest number of seizures in the following thirty days would win the pot.

On the very last day, this guy was hanging around the municipal shuffleboard courts. It was fifteen minutes before noon, which was the end of the contest, and he was one heart attack lower than the highest score. Suddenly an old man dropped his stick. He clutched at his chest and went into spasms. This immediately put the kid in a tie position. At least he would be able to split the kitty. But then, in the confusion and the panic, the outcries and the shuffling of feet, another old man stepped up and grabbed the victim in his arms, trying to keep him from falling. The kid had witnessed a double heart attack. He won the whole pot.

1 Miami Beach. Two million tourists every year. Yachts. Night clubs. Bikinis. Palms. Cadillacs. Sunshine. But there are also 87,-000 permanent residents. The average age is 65.2. Most of them are Jews. Most of them were born in the old country. Most of them live on Social Security, far below the poverty level.

South Beach is where the town started. The years went by, the wars, the inventions. Progress marched away to the north. Hotels became bigger and more lavish. Mansions were constructed. Islands were dredged out of Biscayne Bay. Causeways. Thruways. Motels. Traffic. The Fontainebleau. The Eden Roc. Gradually, South Beach became old-fashioned, then marginal, and finally a slum.

Below Lincoln Road it is all stucco and tile roofs and Mediterranean styles. Or it is flat roofs and cubistic balconies, glass bricks and round corners in the style that couldn't possibly be called anything else but *"moderne."* It is all lime green and sun-bleached pink and turquoise and washed-out blue and apartment houses with names like Aloha, Parkedge, Elaine, Jem Arms, Avon House, and Esplanade.

An old woman is in a wheelchair being pushed up the sidewalk by a young black girl. She holds a cigarette in her upraised fingers as though shushing for silence, her head turned at an angle. She smiles and listens very carefully. But is it the wind rustling through the palms? Or is she listening to the blare of radios, the jets overhead, the neighbors sitting on the front porches fenced in by slats of jalousie windows? Or are there still other voices, inflected with hard accents, softened by the humid air and the shadows, by time and memory, still explaining how hard it all is, how crooked it all is, how impossible to make sense, to make justice, to make a dollar?

Another woman is carrying a shopping bag emblazoned with a map of—and with the word—FLORIDA. She is wearing a leopardskin fabric jacket. She has a leopardskin scarf. Her feet shuffle on the sidewalk. She wears sunglasses. She has no hips at all, and her stockings hang shapelessly on her thin, straight calves. As she passes a large hibiscus bush a cat jumps out. She stops and turns and begins talking to it.

Temple Beth Raphael. The front of the building is covered with mosaics and with plastic tablets.

"Remember what the Amalek of our time did to you. He cut off the lives of six million Jewish souls. Men, women and children, helpless and defenseless."

There is a plaque recently put up as an addenda, dedicated in memoriam to nine Jews hanged in Iraq.

Another street. A woman is dressed in a loose and baggy pants suit of solid red. She carries a red purse. She has red beads, red lipstick, red frames on her sunglasses. She wears a red hat decorated with pink flowers of colored linen.

Next to the bay there is a short row of new, luxury, high-rise condominium apartments. It is a signal. The big real-estate interests are trying to buy up the South Beach area and commit urban renewal. The land would be worth jillions to the real-estate freaks. But they are constantly thwarted by the intense resistance and the political solidarity of the old ones.

Lincoln Road is a showcase. It has been closed to automobiles and converted into a shopping mall for pedestrians. The mall begins at Alton Road and runs east to Washington Avenue. It starts with a cluster of banks, the American Savings and Loan Association decorated with mosaic murals on the outside walls. One of them depicts a moonwalk. Around the corner are murals of the White House, Mount Vernon, the raising of the flag on Iwo Jima, Betsy Ross, and Abraham Lincoln.

During the day you can stroll along past the royal palms, the coconuts, the areca palms and sabal palms, the hibiscus and the oleander, the fountains with colored lights, reflecting pools, dracaenas of every kind, orchids both vanda and radicans, bromeliads, lilies, large boulders and fine gravel, low walls, benches, fan palms, wax palms, paurotis palms, beaucarneas, lantanas, begonias, geraniums, ixoras and crotons. There is a loudspeaker on every corner roof soothing you with Muzak. There are tailor shops, radio and TV shops, antique shops, arts and crafts centers, movie houses, jewelers, dress shops, shoe stores, gift shops, Lane Bryant, realtors, U.S. Army recruiting, a church, travel agency, furriers, art galleries, hair stylists, an automated post-office substation, restaurants, leather-goods stores, Andrew Geller, Walston and Company, and Saks Fifth Avenue. The mall ends with Woolworth's and another bank, the Financial Federal, looming up over a dozen stories high with a flashing sign announcing the time and the temperature.

The stores are all closed by five or six. The shoppers are gone. There is a lull, the mall almost empty. And then after dinner, at sunset, the old ones come out, the poor ones, enjoying the tropical exotica, the wealth, the displays, the soothing music. If the wind is calm and the sky is clear and there is no chill, you can see them strolling or just sitting on the benches, on the rims of the fountains and the pools. They flirt. Their hands keep moving, their faces re-enacting emotions, expressing conviction, outrage, cynicism, humor. The men favor sports jackets in checks and plaids and always with some kind of golf cap. The women wear wigs protected by scarves.

Sit on a bench. Listen. A harsh, strident and lilting voice will saw away at the murmurs, the tints and the reflections, the darkness and the humidity. One woman is explaining it all to another:

"She's got a lovely figure, and she says she wants to be friends with me. You never can tell. Sometimes you meet some very nice people that way. I says to her, "You don't know anything about me. What if I'm a *goniff?*' And she says to me, 'You don't look like a *goniff.*' Oh, you'll love her. She's such a lovely person. You'll sit around and you'll tell her all your sad stories. She's a good listener. Really. And then she'll tell you all her sad stories."

6:10 A.M. The sky is getting light. The running lights of a southbound tanker are visible offshore. The temperature is 75. The moderate breeze feels fresh and cool. The coconuts rustle. A few isolated figures move through the streets. A bald, heavy man wearing a short-sleeve shirt and baggy, knee-length shorts comes walking along Lummus Park. He wears white socks and blue tennis shoes. He has an elastic bandage around his knee. At the fishing pier he marches from one end to the other. Briskly, methodically, he does it a dozen times.

Six men are fishing at the end of the pier. On the beach there is a dory, a lifeguard stand and several shelters made in the Seminole chickee style with four posts and roofs of thatched palms. A man moves along the high-water line very slowly. He carries a metal detector and a net-shaped sieve. He sweeps the handle back and forth, stops, sifts the sand, and then continues back and forth. The pelicans and the gulls fly offshore. There are a few sandpipers. An old lady strolls along the surf in a bathing suit.

7:00 A.M. Between Eighth Street and Ninth Street on the dry sand behind a lifeguard station, twenty-two people are running in place. They bend over, twist and stretch. A man in red shorts runs backward a hundred feet and then returns. A tan woman in a pink bathing suit does the same thing as her very large breasts jiggle and flop. Rise up on your toes. Hands on hips. Twist around. Semaphore with the arms. Stand on one foot and stretch, one arm pointed upward. A man comes jogging up the beach and joins the group.

Harry Margolis is lean and wiry. He wears an undershirt and red plaid shorts. He joined the group fifteen years ago when he retired as a tailor. He is now over eighty and has been the leader for the last four or five years, ever since the previous leader got tired of getting up early. They meet every day, rain or shine, the same place and the same time. One man is over ninety years old. Most are in their seventies.

Margolis has created his own forty-five-minute program, a heavy emphasis on stretching, staying limber and balanced. It is a mishmash of routines that he has gleaned from here and there. "A little yoga. A few things on radio and TV. But not too much strain and not too many times."

They stand on one foot and swing the other leg. Some of them totter. Some lose their balance. A man wears a golf cap. A woman wears a blue nylon scarf over her hair. There is a wooly hat. A bonnet. Long pants and no shirt. Plaid shorts, bathing suits and house dresses, skirts and blouses. They turn their heads and push their chins around with one hand. They take a deep breath and throw their arms back.

One, two. One, two. Rotate one arm with your hand on your shoulder. Run in place. Run backward. Touch your toes. One, two. Squat down. Kick. Bend. Rotate your head. One, two. Hold one ankle behind you and stand on one foot. Raise your other arm aloft. Now hold it. Clasp and unclasp your fingers. Clench your fists.

But some of them can't do it. As others trot, some stay in one place and scarcely move. As some make swimming motions with their arms, one woman dog-paddles. Another can hardly move at all. A bare-chested, bald man in green trousers, with pale skin, stands behind the lifeguard stand. He faces away from all the others, but he works very hard.

No one is quite sure what causes people to get old. But they do know that your bones become brittle and light. Your joints become stiff. Your muscles will be stringy, slower to move, stiffer and weaker and with less endurance. Your bladder will be weaker, your tendons wasted. Your skin will become wrinkled and flabby. It will lose its color and be covered with blotches. You will be susceptible to cold but also to excessive heat. You lose your sense of smell and taste, and there will be less saliva in your mouth. Your digestion will be poor. Your kidneys won't work so well. The lens of the eye becomes hardened and more opaque, which means you will become farsighted, at least. The diameter of the pupil decreases, and you will be more susceptible to glare. The iris fades and the cornea thickens. Blood cells atrophy. So do nerve cells. You will lose your hearing, especially the higher tones. The loss will be even greater if you are a man, especially in your left ear. Your nose will gradually get much larger than it is now. So will your ear lobes. Your perceptions won't be as sharp and as clear. You will become less sensitive to sugar. And to salt. But you will be more sensitive to pain. Your posture will be as poor as your sense of balance, and this will make you prone to accidents. Your voice will get higher and weaker, your breathing poor. You will have circulation problems— varicose veins, cholesterol in the arteries, malfunctioning of the heart. Your reaction time will get slower. You will suffer loss of brain cells. The thyroid gland gets smaller and less active. The adrenals begin to shrink. Your hair will turn gray and then white. If you are lucky. Otherwise you will lose it all. You will gradually suffer from gum diseases, and one by one you will lose your teeth. Your memory will go bad, especially for recent events. You will have less and less sex, although a little variety sometimes prolongs the process—new habits and new partners. But the ovaries will cease functioning between the ages of forty-five and fifty-five. The breasts will dry up. So will the uterus and the vagina. Hormone production will go into decline. The metabolism will slow down. You are bound to gain weight. A thirty-year-old man who weighs 154 pounds and who eats the same amount and continues to do the same work which was enough to burn up all the calories will nevertheless weigh 209 pounds by the time he is sixty-two.

Meanwhile, you aren't making as much money. Your friends have all died. Your family has grown up, disappeared or scattered. You are alone. Young people avoid you. And you have nothing to do.

But as the sun comes out of the low clouds at 7:13, the breeze is fresh and the sea is green. The beach is nearly deserted. There are twenty-four of you now. Independent strollers pass up and down the line of surf. Pigeons hobble on the sand among the thatched chickees and the wire baskets and all those signs saying "No."

Clap your hands in unison. Squeeze and massage your wrists. And then your arms. Ankles. Calves. Put your hands behind your back, clench fingers and pull. Knead the small of your back, your shoulder blades.

The coconut palms are scrawny and wind-whipped, yellow from the dry winter and the cold. There is no traffic on the street. Only a few people watch from the benches in the park.

7:43 A.M. They pick up sandals, purses, papers and towels and walk over the deep sand with slow and awkward feet. Small groups are formed. Subgroups. Cou-

ples. Singles. People talk. Each goes his own way. Some
sit on benches and wipe the sand off their feet. They put
on shoes and sandals and cross Ocean Drive.

Noon. The beach is crowded. It is nearly 90 degrees
and very humid. People sit on aluminum lawn chairs or
stretch out on the sand on towels or on the grass of
Lummus Park, ignoring the "Keep Off" signs. Their
skins are dark and gleaming with oil. Or they are white
with blue veins and curdles of fat as they sit in the shade
of a pandanus tree and read the paper. Ships are on the
horizon, fishing boats closer in. A helicopter goes by a
few hundred yards offshore. An extremely fat woman
laughs in the distance, raucous, short, repeated like the
cry of a gull. Spanish is being spoken on all sides. Polish.
Yiddish. The accents of New York.

And then the sirens, the lights, the red and white van.
An old and heavy woman sitting on a chair in the shade
is in distress. The fire department's Mobile Emergency
Care Unit stops at the curb. The Miami Beach Patrol
arrives. The firemen and the doctor talk to her. They
examine her. One stands up and glares at the curious.
"All right. Stand back everybody. This lady doesn't
want you to stand around and stare at her."

DINE OUT TONIGHT PICCIOLO REST. SINCE 1936 GARDEN
ROOM. 2ND ST. COLLINS M.B.

The sign is being towed behind a very slow airplane
flying low just off the beginning of the breaking surf. It
heads north. The rescue unit leaves. The woman is still
in her chair being fussed over by an old man with a big
paunch.

Sunglasses. Bonnets. Plastic nose guards attached to the bridge of sunglasses. Card games under the shade of a coconut palm. Hair curlers. A tall, bewhiskered, once muscular man is sitting on a bench wearing ragged cutoffs and a tee shirt. His hair is long and thinning, grayish blond. He is drunk. A torn black plastic handbag beside him is filled with bread rolls and odds and ends. His head lolls, and crumbs fall out of his mouth as he chews. He wears thong sandals, his ankles and feet badly swollen.

Two women sit side by side in aluminum chairs at the very edge of the ocean, letting the surf roll in over their feet. Without their noticing, the chairs are gradually sinking down into the sand. A skinny old lady in a bathing suit and a basket hat is lying on her stomach on top of the low stone wall, propped up on her elbows. Her skin is darkly tanned and wrinkled. She talks to herself softly, her eyes empty. The back of her suit is unzipped and falls away from her shoulders. Her breasts dangle visibly.

Pigeons. Sparrows. A wheelchair. An old man is fast asleep with his mouth open, lying on his back in the full sun. A woman stands alone on the sand, facing the sea. She is doing slow-motion calisthenics. The sky is clear. It is hot. Jascha Heifetz is playing his violin over a portable radio. A woman wears a small eyeshade of opaque plastic, biting a scrap of Saran Wrap that covers her lips. People play canasta on a square of masonite. To keep the cards from blowing away, there is a crisscross arrangement of twine and a dozen small stones.

Somewhat young, short-haired, his body speaking the language of evangelism, a man stands on the lawn waving a New Testament, speaking of his own sins and of forsaking Christ. Twisting, bending, stretching, he waves his arms as he gesticulates with the Bible, his voice lifting with emphasis, hard with its dedication. Fourteen Jews sit on their lawn chairs in silence. They knit. They read the paper. They stare at him glumly or look away with embarrassment. Far enough away so he can't be heard, a man talks out loud to anybody, to you, to him, it doesn't matter.

"Let 'im talk. He's entitled to his opinion. A lot of Jews down here wanna throw 'im out. But let 'im talk. He's got a right. The President, he's always talkin'. Right? About this and that. And now look. That bum. They oughta hang 'im from a tree. Watergate? Are you kiddin' me?"

Go to the Social Security office. Get some pamphlets. Take a numbered tag and sit down. Wait. People go in and come out. Numbers are called by the white-haired clerk at the desk. The inner door opens and closes and a woman comes out.

"That's some rude woman you sent me in to see. Rude! Rude!"

"Whaddaya want me to do? I got nothin' to do with what goes on in there."

"Never mind all that. You should save your energy and do something about the situation."

"Wha'? Wha'? She's senior to me. I'm not her boss. She's *my* boss. Whaddaya want me to say to the boss?"

Go to Liggett's drugstore on Lincoln Road Mall. Diet scales are given a prominent display in the windows.

There are piles of portable electric broilers, toasters and hot plates. Just inside the side door can be seen several stacks of Sunsweet prune juice. The cardboard cases are cut open, the green bottles ready to go.

Walk down Washington Avenue. The post office is here, city hall, podiatrists' offices, clinics, medical centers, optometrists, bargain stores, discount drugstores. You can see a double feature here for seventy-five cents. Kosher meat markets. Kosher hotels. A sign: CUBAN SEPHARDIC HEBREW CONGREGATION. At most of the clinics the doctors' names are Spanish. A flock of very old women is sitting on a bench at the corner, waiting for a bus. Every hundred feet there is a large prominent sign in red and white: NO JAY WALKING—$3.00 FINE.

And still they cross in every direction, in mid-block, heads down, shuffling, slow, oblivious. At the Thrifty Super Market it is a free-for-all of shopping carts snarled in every aisle. They crash into one another. They are double-parked, abandoned, forgotten. At Richard's Fruit Center, at Big Chips and at Fruitco, they shop in the old European manner. Every piece of fruit is mauled and handled, squeezed and judged. Piles of vegetables are turned over and over, seeking that one which is the biggest, the ripest, the best before putting it into a bag. Signs warn against shoplifting. The cashiers have wary eyes.

At city hall the sign says CITIZENS SERVICE BUREAU. It also says BUREAU DE SERVICIOS CIUDADANDOS. And it also says it in Hebrew. At S.H. Kress & Co. you can get irregular nylon hose for twenty-seven cents, and you can save ninety-seven cents on your choice of $1.99 shower curtains and $1.39 scatter rugs. A theater marquee advertises ON STAGE—YIDDISH AMERICAN VAUDEVILLE. Cotton dresses are on sale at a bargain store. There is a crowd up the street. A red and white van is parked at the curb, the emergency lights flashing. A doctor and two young drivers are writing reports and putting away equipment. A man stands by the plate-glass window. There is dirt on the back of his jacket, and he has a wan smile. One woman is stridently explaining to another:

"The doctor checked him up two days ago. He says there is nothing *wrong.*"

She tries to give two dollars to the driver. He smiles and shakes his head. The crowd mutters its curiosity, its reassurances. There are hippies in the crowd. A Cadillac with New York tags is parked at the curb. Farther on there is a cluster of people in front of the Governor Cafeteria. An old man with a thin gray beard sits on the fender of a parked Continental. His shoulders are slumped. A shopping bag is on the curbstone. His shoes are without laces, bulging and worn out. His socks have collapsed. The grimy legs of long-handled underwear are showing beneath his trouser cuffs. A fedora hat is held upside down on his thigh.

At the cafeteria a woman hobbles up to the cash register with a cane, a crippled hip, and large dark spots on her wrists, her hands twisted grotesquely with arthritis. A counterman comes around when the cashier calls him to carry the woman's tray. An ugly, slovenly old woman at a table is hunched over her plate. She has never quite learned the table manners of northern Europe. She gets it in any old way, left hand or right hand, stick it in and chomp it up, lips smacking loudly.

The rest of the clientele is old and defeated, with a

smattering of the half old and the half defeated. The plastic begins with the floors and the furniture. It goes up the walls and over the ceiling and drips stalactites of plastic signs, plastic flowers and plastic birds to go with the plastic food. A sign: NOSHVILLE, U.S.A.

In the back of McCrory's, next to Section 9, "Glassware and Kitchen Needs," a man sits somberly at a table with a sphygmomanometer, a stethoscope, and a cash register. Behind him is a wall of plastic flowers and plastic fruits. Four people are waiting their turns, sitting on hard folding chairs. Three more are standing. All are serious and silent. You wait. You sit. You get the cuff wrapped around your arm. The bulb is squeezed, the pressure increased. The nut is gradually loosened as the man listens, looks at the aneroid dial, nods, unwraps you, writes two numbers on a slip of paper. You give him your dollar. He rings it up. You leave. The windows just outside are loaded with displays of kids' beach balloons. There is Pluto and Donald Duck and Dumbo. Thermos jugs. Styrofoam cooler chests. Silk-screened souvenir beach towels from Miami Beach, Florida.

The woman's pressure is 130/75. It's normal. Happily she laughs and asks you to guess her age. Say, sixty-seven. She replies:

"I'm seventy-six. But don't tell my boyfriend."

Those who have high blood pressure always resist the idea of seeing a doctor. Staring at the penciled systolic and diastolic numbers, they claim they have been unusually nervous all day. Or they had too much coffee. Or they were rushing around too much in this heat. The customers are not hypochondriacs. Ninety-five percent of them do have high blood pressure. They are regulars and they are scared. All of them are on "pressure pills," but none of them will stay on a diet. If they feel a little dizzy in the morning, they immediately run for a test.

"One hundred seventy-two? That's good. No? I'm eighty-three next month. You're supposed to be a hundred plus your age."

"Oh. Please. Please. Not again. That makes no sense at all. That means a baby should have a blood pressure of one hundred? If you're ninety years old it should be one-ninety?

A man's systolic reads two-hundred. He is sweating. Quietly he is told to rest awhile. In a few more minutes he will do it over. The mailman comes in.

"Where's Lew?"

"His brother passed away. He went to New York. I'm covering for him until he comes back Monday."

The regular man is a retired doctor who runs the concession. His replacement is a chiropractor. He wanted to play golf today but doesn't even have time for lunch, chewing on a sandwich as he works, the line of customers almost constant.

They are in their seventies and eighties. They are terribly afraid of having a stroke and especially of being trapped in their rooms, alone. The dime-store blood-pressure business sprang up as an economic necessity. Doctors jack up the prices, prolong treatments, create needless return visits. Often they will charge much more than Medicare allows, and then the patient must make up the difference. He already has to pay 20 percent of the cost as it is.

A woman approaches the doctor, whirling an onion chopper over her head in frenzied circles.

"How much *is* this? There's no price on it."

Go over to Granny's Sundries on Collins Avenue. Fannie Reichgott is seventy-seven. On the wall of her eleven-foot-wide store is an official occupational license issued for "letter writing." She charges thirty-five cents for two pages written by hand and fifty cents if it's typewritten. She does ten a day in the winter, a lot of them love letters. But she refuses business letters. The biggest problem is playing psychologist. You can't write down exactly what people tell you. One old man was cursing his daughter in Yiddish, but of course she translated it all into benign euphemisms. His daughter was the one who sent the checks. When Fannie went on vacation, another woman filled in for her. But this woman wrote the letter just as the man dictated it, word for word. It wasn't easy, but Fannie managed to straighten out the chaos when she returned.

Summer is the slow season. The illiterates who correspond all have families to write to. Therefore they tend to be the more affluent in the neighborhood, and most of them go north for vacation. At least one of them has to check into a hotel because there is never "enough room" at the very house she bought for her son. But what can you do with parents who were born on the other side, who are illiterate, who speak broken English with horrible accents, who were mutilated by generations of malnutrition—bowed legs, short stature, obesity—who can talk only about relatives, gossip and money and their own agonies, real or imagined? And you are a member of the board at the country club?

They all seem to come in at once. If someone is seen getting a letter read or having one written in reply, they all want one. Most are from Russia. They can't read English, and their children don't understand Yiddish.

Fannie's father came from the Hungary of Franz Josef, an educated man who spoke ten languages. It all started with the volunteer work she used to do at Kingsbridge Veterans Hospital in Brooklyn, writing letters for the basket cases or the men with no hands.

Fanny talks a mile a minute. She gripes about land-lords, the women in the neighborhood who are drunks, the peanuts-and-cookie delivery man with the black wife who has problems and who overcharged them $1.28 on the last delivery, about her son the jazz musician, the son who went to Korea, the other one in the Navy during World War II, how spoiled the kids are today but "thank God" they can be, her great-granddaughter who was adopted, her husband's father from Poland who spoke five languages, about show business, her son who plays the bass fiddle, the days she attended the New England Conservatory, playing the piano, the neighborhood kids who always try to walk through the store from the back alley to take a short cut, the alcoholic women she has tried to help by putting clothes on them and food in their belly and then the next time she sees them they are drunk again; sometimes it's a regular skid row around here; well, no, maybe she didn't really graduate from the conservatory; she shouldn't say that; she attended. And that's her daughter up there in the picture on the wall standing next to Milton Berle. She's in show business too.

Her husband comes back from the bank, furious. She forgot to endorse the Social Security check.

In Flamingo Park the men are arguing politics under the banyan tree. Some of them are radical Socialists.

Some of them are anti-Zionists. Other old men are watching dirty movies in the theater on 21st Street and Collins Avenue where the sign says: "The story of intercourse—educational—not pornographic." Others are playing cards or playing shuffleboard at one of the city's recreation centers. They take night courses at the high school. They *kvetch* and they *kibbitz*. They make ceramics. They go to the temple. They learn folk dancing. They take mandolin lessons.

Four people sitting on a bench:

"She's only gonna be here a couple of days."

"Yeah. That's right."

"I'm tryin' to convince her she should stay longer."

"So. What else is new here?"

An old lady shuffling her feet:

"Damp. Damp. Too damp. Too damp here. We can't stay in Florida. It's damp. Damp."

Evening. There is a small area in Lummus Park where there are rows of bright-orange benches. The old ones begin to gather—ugly and fat, white-haired and bald, tottering, worn out, staring, drooling, weak. They carry pillows. They bring their canes and their hearing aids. There are accented murmurs, the drag and shuffle of feet. A silent couple no more than five feet tall go by holding hands.

A flag is fluttering at the top of a steel pole. At the base is a small shopping cart stolen from some supermarket. It holds a cheap portable microphone, a small American flag, and an Israeli flag on sticks. One by one the volunteers stagger up and are introduced by the master of ceremonies. Reluctantly or with bravado, they begin to sing. Without any music and with cracked, hoarse, faltering voices, they sing those old songs from the *shtetl*. When somebody hits on an old favorite, there is a low, murmuring chant from the crowd.

Their backs are turned to the Atlantic Ocean, whispering behind them. They are facing the sun as it sets amid the silhouettes of coconut palms, black and lacy, brushing over the colors. And they all remember being kids back in Russia. They remember wrapping their bare feet in rags to go out in the snow. They weren't allowed to attend the public schools. They couldn't own land. Isolated in their villages, they never even learned to speak proper Russian.

They remember those old songs. And they remember the cattle boats and the stink and the seasickness. They can tell you about holding their mother's hand as she stood on deck by the rail, crying and watching the Statue of Liberty. And about Ellis Island in the early 1900s, about the Lower East Side, Brooklyn, the Bronx, about working fourteen hours a day, their son the doctor and their son the lawyer making it and moving on to Cadillac City, where they get a postcard from every six months and maybe a check on Chanukah.

A jet roars over their heads, aimed into the prevailing wind, then slowly swinging wide and heading north.

But they sing. They are retired, living in still another ghetto, the slum of the Great American Paradise. But at least they are not freezing their *tuchis* every winter. And they don't find swastikas painted on the temple doors or on the tombstones of their dead.

Afterward, if it is Sunday, Monday or Friday, they can

go to Friendship Corner #1 down by the fishing pier. There is a simple square proscenium of cement blocks painted green. There is a stage, a cheap p.a. system, another American flag, and more of the orange benches. Fishermen stroll by. Hippies cruise. People walk their dogs. Cubans *oye* and *mira* around. The surf can be heard on both sides, washing over the sand.

Solemnly the crowd listens to the old ladies singing tuneless old ballads without music but with grandiose gestures. The M.C. introduces them in a mixture of half English and half Yiddish. There are gypsy songs and then "Oh, how I hate to get up in the morning." Next to the flag stands a senile man with a protruding belly, his toothless mouth sagging open with an expression of empty pleasure. One arm is missing. In his remaining hand he shakes some weird, vibrating musical instrument that makes a whining, metallic percussion sound. He controls the tone with his fingers.

On a chair against the wall slumps a mandolin player, his instrument forgotten in his lap. His face is empty, his eyes staring at nothing, understanding at last the vacancy of all things.

In the audience sits an alert and handsome woman of seventy-odd, wearing a necklace, earrings, her best dress. She is alone. Nearby, a man holds his chin on his hand, staring over the railing at the void of the night and the sea where a small light is glowing on the horizon.

9:05 P.M. They sing "God Bless America" and then the Israeli national anthem. They leave in a group, going down the pier together, their shoes making a distinct shuffling sound that blends with the surf and the hissing of the foam. To the north are the lights of the hotels and

night clubs. Barely obscured to the south is Key Biscayne, the residence of President Nixon. Ahead of them
is a longhair leaning on top of a parking meter and the
neck of his guitar.

Through the alleys. Back to Collins Avenue and
beyond. Back to the Nemo Hotel, the Blackstone. Back
to the porches and the TV and the canasta in the lobbies.

Or if it is Thursday you can go to the Pier Park Band-
shell at 8:oo P.M. to see a Walt Disney presentation of a
true-life adventure on Seal Island. The wind is very
strong and chilly. The admission is free. The crowd is
huddled in sweaters and coats, sitting on cushions or on
pallets of newspapers. The coconuts rustle as they learn
all about the Aleutians and the Pribilofs, the music challenged by the wind and by the jets.

But if it is Sunday, Tuesday, Wednesday or Thursday
you can go to the Ocean Front Auditorium at Tenth
Street. The social dance costs twenty-five cents for admission. Suitable attire is required. Dudes stroll in, stiff
and erect, wearing suits and bow ties and cuff links.
Chicks wear tropical prints, clutching their purses, their
hair carefully arranged in ritual patterns. There are
pants suits and lamé jackets, head scarves and cheap
cotton dresses, wedgie shoes, spike heels, old scuffed
Space-Shoes and Capri pants, sequins and slacks, beads,
necklaces, and golf caps. One woman is dressed in a
pseudo-peasant costume, a fantasy of pink and black
boots, ruffled skirts, an embroidered collar, plastic pink
beads and earrings.

The music plays. They dance. Arthur Murray did his
job well. They do the Lambeth Walk. Bossa Nova.
Rumba. Conga. Tango. Old ladies dance with each other.

An old man in a sweater and Keds sneakers and a string tie is sashaying around.

There are gold diggers here, shack jobs who just might end up splitting with the pension checks, the silver and the sheets. It happens all the time. But there is also affection here, an easing of those lingering sexual hungers, the comfort of being with your peers who know what it is to be considered ludicrous by a world that has no patience for the lover encumbered by canes, wigs, corsets, dentures, trusses and supports. This world knows there is something terribly obscene about grandma making out down on the beach, the wind tearing at her babushka, some dirty old man fooling around under her skirts. And the guy would never marry her. As a couple they would lose part of their Social Security money.

The French doors open onto a patio and walled courtyard. Colored lights are strung up the trunks of coconut palms and among the branches of the sea grapes. A dozen couples go outside to dance in the open air. The girls have blue hair and spit curls and lipstick free-formed over the area where lips used to be. They do the fox trot and the waltz and they do it very slowly, with pirouettes and dips and swirls that are not graceful now and never were but are instead rather smug and stiff and prissy.

And yet, hanging over the top of the walls are bell-bottomed, bare-chested teenagers with long hair, and young adults with middle hair, and tanned lifeguards with short hair. And not a son of a bitch moves nor smiles nor says a god damn word.

Away from the beach you can stroll through the alleys and the apartment-house courtyards and look through the open windows at the cheap furniture, the gewgaws and souvenirs, the rock from Canada, the bottle of black sand from Hawaii, the reproductions of sentimental mountain scenes, the photos of families, the grand-children at their bar-mitzvahs, the plastic this and the plastic that hanging on the wall. There is a gray head wearing a black yarmulka in the kitchen. There are fans in the windows. The rooms are neat and clean and very, very small.

Everywhere there is electronic sound. Every window flickers with a blue and white light. The same situation comedy is magnified by the nearly empty rooms without drapes that act as echo chambers. Dim figures doze in their chairs, unaware of the din.

And then you realize you have been observing only the strong ones, the healthy and the active. But there are also those who never go out at all.

Late at night they sit on the front porches of their rooming houses. They watch the moon landings on television. They stare out at the quiet streets, the air hot and sticky, the traffic very light. They sit on folding chairs in straight rows, motionless, their faces blue in the fluorescent lights. These are the survivors, packed on a string of square life rafts, drifting on a flat, perpetual sea that has no tide. And they are waiting. They are still waiting.

The deserted parking lot at the Food Fair market at Fifth and Washington has an illuminated billboard that spells out a forlorn message in movable plastic letters:

LOOK WHAT TEN CENTS CAN BUY.

Silhouettes of passing traffic blur the words. Headlights flare. Cars turn the corner with an accelerating roar. The message is pale and unread in the silence and in the reflected green and pink and in the blackness of the night. On the other side of the sign is the answer:

FIVE POUNDS OF SUNSHINE SUGAR.

* * *

He was seventy-eight. After he retired he spent twenty years betting the horses every day. When he died of a heart attack they found a dozen large paper bags in his room, filled with old ticket stubs. In accordance with his sealed instructions, his son and daughter scattered his ashes at the track at Hialeah. It took a while to find the right place. His son opened the package, took out the cardboard box, scooped out the fragments of bone with his hand and scattered them over a bed of caladiums. With each toss, a swarm of small moths rose up in a nervous cloud.

* * *

She was a doctor. Both she and her husband were osteopaths, were witty, sophisticated, and socially prominent. Suddenly, he died of a heart attack. Their daughter had a congenital kidney problem. Her behavior became erratic. She took drugs. She began to lose patients. One day they found three suicide notes written on her prescription blanks. She had taken an overdose of sedatives. Her nine-year-old daughter was dead from chloroform, peacefully clutching her doll in her arms. But the woman was still breathing. She was revived but remembered nothing. Charged with murder, she became hysterical and had to be chained to her bed. She refused medical care and nearly died. She made two attempts to escape, again tried to kill herself, and again almost died. She was committed to a mental hospital, where she lived another thirty-five years. Her estate was unclaimed—a Social Security card and a gold wedding ring. She had had one visitor. She was eighty-three.

2 She was quite pleasant on the telephone and gracious with her invitation. But she didn't want her name to be used. She wasn't really sure why, but she had seen that television documentary about the old people on the Lower East Side of New York. She remembered the terrified old man who always waited in the foyer for somebody to go up in the elevator with him. In the previous three years he had been mugged and knifed five times. And she too had been robbed. A few years ago, during a bad hurricane, she had gone up north, visiting her old home on Long Island. A neighbor was keeping an eye on her place in Florida, but still, about $9,000 worth of valuables were stolen. They took her jewelry, her sables and mink, her silver. They also took most of her souvenirs from France, where she had driven an ambulance during World War I.

She was seventy-nine. She came from Pottsville, Pennsylvania. Her mother, who lived to be eighty-six, was very English and was related to a lord. John O'Hara went to school with her sister, and his father had been their family doctor. She didn't approve of O'Hara's books because she thought he portrayed the people of Pottsville as being nothing but hicks. She still had a photograph of her volunteer medical group marching down the main street, two of them carrying an empty stretcher, all of them in uniform, the men wearing puttees. And there she was, pretty, young, fresh and strong, proudly wearing her overseas cap, a uniform jacket, and very long skirts. But in France everyone was shocked when they learned her family name. It was classic Pennsylvania Dutch, and in those days the anti-German feeling was very strong.

She drove a Dodge ambulance that her father had donated to the Red Cross. She made several runs from Paris to Château-Thierry right after the battle and also served at Belleau Wood and near Verdun. Then she was sent to Brest. The troopships all had a draft greater than thirty-four feet and therefore had to anchor out, the soldiers coming ashore on lighters and barges. Afterward, the wounded were ferried out and put on board. She and two other aides were in charge of loading a total of 60,000.

She remembered one particular lighter that carried out twenty-five special cases. All of them were quadruple amputees, moaning and cursing in protest at being forcibly sent home in their condition, many of them in tears, pleading with the orderlies to roll them over the side.

But every six weeks she got a furlough and could go to Paris and have fun and forget things like the ship that arrived with four thousand troops, four hundred of them already dead from influenza, or the desperate stowaways who hid among the wounded. In Paris she met General Pershing. She met President and Mrs. Wilson on two different occasions.

She also met her future husband, a psychiatrist and a captain in the medical corps. After the war he worked at the state hospital for the criminally insane at Dannemora, New York, and then opened a private general hospital on Long Island which he operated for twenty-one years. In 1940 they were divorced. He went back into the Army during World War II and emerged a lieutenant colonel. In 1956 he died.

That was the same year she moved to Florida and bought a home. She used to travel a great deal, but now she wanted peace and quiet. Except for one possible last trip to Spain and Portugal.

She never remarried and had no children. In a quiet voice, averting her eyes and speaking in a husky monotone, she began the story of how the son of her ex-husband's second wife spent years searching for her. He called up one day after many frustrated hunts and asked if he could come over and visit. He asked for any mementos she might have of his father. He had often asked his parents about her, but nobody wanted to tell him anything. "Of course, I knew why," she said. And her mouth formed a hard line, her chin trembling. Even after thirty-two years the faint traces of that ancient anguish lingered in the room, the echoes of a long-dead treachery, a breach of faith. There was betrayal there. There was adultery.

She lived alone. She had a white Cadillac in the driveway. She ate all her meals out but made sure she got home before dark. She never went out in the evening except when in the company of visitors. A maid came in to clean. She went out every day to visit and to care for her cousin who was a patient at a nearby psychiatric nursing home. She was her cousin's legal guardian and felt very responsible, her obligation of honor keeping her very busy, once again her nursing instinct bringing out her need for sacrifice and for service. It was not a matter of having something to do. It was a vocation.

Her feelings about contemporary life were mixed and undecided. She favored most of the current technology but wasn't sure which kind. She was certainly pleased by the advances in space travel and approved of the moon walks. But she was appalled by the moral disintegration of the last ten to fifteen years. Very quickly she became agitated, her words coming faster, her lips drawing into a hard line. All of it, the hedonism, the abortions, the general permissiveness, it made her think of the "fall of Rome." She was "heartsick and very discouraged" by the conduct of America's youth during the last ten years. All that dope. All that promiscuity. She was very much against the eighteen-year-old vote. She thought television should be monitored by a committee appointed by President Nixon in order to screen out the excess violence. She had once met Nixon, and she approved of him completely. She was against smoking marijuana. She was against pornography. She agreed with a friend who wanted to leave the country. But she wasn't sure which country she wanted to go to. Not France—but England, perhaps.

Vietnam was certainly a mistake, she said. But the

U.S. should have gone in all the way and used atomic weapons.

Her voice became higher and stronger as she spoke of the Army deserters in Sweden and the draft dodgers in Canada. People should always be willing to fight for their country. Back in France, in 1917, the seasoned volunteer troops stood on the docks and jeered at those fresh arrivals who actually had to be drafted into the Army.

And then with tight lips and quickened breath:

"Disloyalty. I can't stand disloyalty. That's the very reason I divorced my husband."

She was seventy-one. Her son was thirty-eight. When he died she was too feeble to call for help. Nearly a week later a neighbor telephoned police, complaining about the smell. They found the man's body on the bed in advanced decomposition. His mother was huddled on the floor of the bathroom. Very faintly, she called:

  "I'm over here."

＊　＊　＊

3 Manor Pines—a plastic colonial mansion. Fluted hollow columns. Phony antique brick. The lobby was very large and spacious, with traditional junk furniture and plants both real and artificial: monsteras, philodendrons, and geraniums. The music, piped in from hidden speakers, was interrupted by a news program. With the everyday hysterics of radio, the announcer repeated that morning's newspaper story of the helpless woman discovered with the rotting body of her dead son. The announcer went on with other news.

A middle-aged woman stood at the receptionist's desk. As she asked for an application form she reached behind her to pull down her girdle. The music resumed. An elderly nurse entered the front door in a crisp white uniform, leading a tottering old woman by the hand.

"Hi, guy."

It was Ralph Marrinson, who looked and sounded like

the man in the TV commercial whom you see through the mirror of the medicine cabinet. He was thirty-two, the chairman of the Florida Council for Nursing Home Administrators.

Statistics:

Ten percent of the population of the United States is over sixty-five. In Florida it is 14.5 percent. In Alaska it is 2.2 percent. In any nursing home 90 percent of the patients are over sixty-five. Seventy percent are over seventy-five. Fifty percent are over seventy-seven. Thirty-three percent are over eighty-five. There are twice as many women patients as there are men. Half of all nursing-home patients are disoriented at least part of the time. Arteriosclerosis is the most common ailment.

There was an enormous pseudo-colonial lantern lying on the shag carpet in Mr. Marrinson's office. They were going to have two of them by the front door of the new building. He took out the architect's drawing and with great enthusiasm explained the theme. It was going to be named Independence Hall, and the emphasis would be on "independence." The home would be in the "limited care" category, with a nurse on twenty-four-hour duty. There would be served meals, but there would also be a fully equipped kitchenette and pantry in every room.

Ralph Marrinson pointed out the extra length of the bathrooms, the grab rails, the several call buttons strategically placed for summoning assistance, the ingenious floor plan that left an open space from door to bedroom so a stretcher could be carried in and out without meeting obstructing partitions.

Mr. Marrinson was very excited, constantly stressing the importance of environment for old people. There would be four different decorator styles in the rooms. He led the way through the incomplete construction, over rough concrete pourings, past stacks of unhung doors. There's where the old-fashioned brick post office would be, the place where the carpet would change to cobblestones, with logs on the walls. It was going to be Main Street, U.S.A. And over here would be the Betsy Ross Room and over there through the picture windows you would be able to see Bunker Hill, a large pile of fill dirt decorated with stones and flowers. It was a geriatric Disneyland.

Eight ladies were playing cards in a corner of the dining room. Their hair and their wigs were all gray, with silver and blue rinses. They all wore lipstick. In another corner was a woman trembling from Parkinson's disease. She looked very old but was in fact fifty-one. Mr. Marrinson said that all nursing-home administrators retire early, as soon as they find themselves caring for their own contemporaries.

The east wing was reserved for the senile and the incontinent. Despite the equipment, the skill, the labor and the standards, there was nevertheless the strong pervading odor of urine. But this was a "good day."

A woman sat in a wheelchair with a catheter and a plastic bag visible under her robe. She was smiling, cheerful and pleasant. A white-haired visitor was sitting next to another woman in a wheelchair. He wore a suit and tie. With great dignity, he was feeding her with a spoon. Another man slumped, his legs sticking out into the hall. He was in the terminal stages of Parkinson's disease, his tremors controlled by heavy doses of L-dopa. They had expected him to die months ago.

Through the doors you could see the wrinkled, mummified forms, the dead stares. One woman was ninety-seven, the victim of a stroke. She weighed seventy pounds, drawn up into a fetal position on the bed, being spoon-fed by a nurse. Others sat in chairs equipped with tray tables like the high chairs of infants. One woman held a teddy bear against her cheek, the palm of her other hand stiff, the fingers aiming at something. Another kept rubbing the surface of her tray. She was sliding out of the chair. She was put back into position, and Marrinson asked about the rubbing.

"It feels good."

Marrinson went into a room, speaking to an emaciated, smiling woman lying in bed.

"I've brought you a visitor."

"Hello, son."

"He's an eligible bachelor."

"What?"

"An eligible bachelor."

"He's gonna go back and eat me?"

"No. An eligible bachelor."

"He's going to come back."

"No. He's . . . an . . . eligible . . . bachelor."

"I don't understand."

"Well. We'll see you later."

"Goodbye, son."

Stories:

A ninety-four-year-old woman broke through the screen of a window in the middle of the night, got out into a field and fell into a pile of construction material.

She emerged unhurt, explaining that her son was out there with a helicopter and was going to give her a ride. A ninety-seven-year-old woman who had never even so much as said "heck" or "darn" suddenly began swearing like a sailor, shocking her own children, trying to attack one of the nurses. A ninety-two-year-old man asked for a private conference to solve a personal problem, afraid that he had made one of the patients pregnant. She was seventy-two. Old people always revert to childhood ways. They acquire toys, they get jealous, they build up sibling rivalries for the attention of the nurses and have puppy-love affairs and infatuations. Birthdays are very important. And so is Halloween. There are cakes and treats, and the nurses change into costumes.

But boredom is not a problem. Neither is death. If two seniles share a room and one of them dies, the other is told he "went home." But if the other roommate is alert he will accept the reality. The process of aging gradually reduces all desires, all appetites, every instinct. The big problems here are with the nursing staff. It is difficult to get productive help with any sense of dependability, and the visiting relatives are always a problem, especially the females, who compete with one another, vying for the title of most-dedicated, most-self-sacrificing, most-concerned. A sense of humor is all-important, depression the occupational disease.

Eight years ago Mrs. Bollinger, the head nurse, was ashamed of admitting she worked in nursing homes. But then came Medicare. Big business invested in the health industry, licensing became strict, supervision controlled. Today Florida ranks among the top twelve of the states in the quality of its nursing homes.

There was a beauty shop and an ice-cream parlor, a physiotherapy room with its bars and exercise chairs, its stretch wheels, walkers and crutches. There were two large patio gardens surrounded by picture windows. There was a total of six husband-and-wife "sets."

In an alcove off the dining room there was the Gold Room. A TV set was on, taped laughter rising and falling as a woman in white uniform, with the cap of a registered nurse, angrily adjusted a knob. "I'm not going to get involved with this TV argument again. It's like the Paris peace talks around here." She stormed away, leaving the crowd of old patients grouped around the set, pouting, confused, peeved. They were in pajamas and bathrobes. They had shawls or blankets over their laps. Most of them sat in wheelchairs. One very old woman was wearing a green eyeshade, the kind once used by dealers in gambling casinos. Somebody wanted the set turned up louder or softer; someone else wanted another channel.

In one of the $50 private rooms a very large and expensive doll sat on a chair.

* * *

She was seventy-five. Her son had kept her locked in a bedroom for over a year, naked, with a sheet wrapped around her, the windows sealed shut. There was excrement all over the room. When the police were admitted they found her hair matted with dirt and dandruff. She had lice. She gulped down ten glasses of water. She was incoherent and didn't know her name. Her son refused to answer questions before talking to his lawyer. Her hands were shaking as they carried her away on a stretcher. She was weeping softly.

* * *

He was forty-two. He braided tropical hats out of fronds and sold them on the beach. Taking off his shoes, he climbed the coconut palm in his yard. But he touched some high tension wires and was killed. When the firemen found him he was hanging upside down, his body rotting. He carried no identification.

* * *

4 Clearwater Beach. An old bungalow painted pink with aluminum awnings. Cabbage palms. Cedar shingles. Private houses built right down on the edge of the sand. A row of crooked casuarinas all bent in the direction of the prevailing wind.

On the pier, two old ladies sat on a bench wearing basket hats and sunglasses. The older wore a sweater. She shifted her false teeth and pointed with her cane. They were born in that part of Hungary which has since become part of Czechoslovakia. Giggling about their ages, they claimed eighteen at first and then changed it to "over seventy" and "over eighty." The younger did most of the talking, her accent hard and heavy.

At first she said they were sisters but then said they were cousins. The older came over in 1920. Things were better in this country. You made more money. They worked in fur coats as machine operators and lived in

Manhattan. It was nice then. They had big buildings and everything. Now? Forget it. Robbery. Locks on the doors. Hit you on the head.

They lived together forty-four years. In 1955 they moved to Florida. They had a nice house. They did all the cleaning and mowed the lawn. It was good exercise. Every morning they prepared lunch and then came out to sit on the pier for two hours. At eleven they went home. They went to bed early. If there was something good on TV they'd watch it. They used to play cards a lot but not so much anymore.

They never had children. They giggled. Sometimes they played a game. I'm your daughter and you're my momma. You know how it is. They were Catholics. Church made them feel good. God helped. But they didn't go to church as much as they used to.

The older woman had made three trips back to Hungary while her mother was still living. But now everybody was gone already, brothers and cousins, everybody. Besides. It cost too much to see relatives. They never married. For what? They had such a nice life and plenty of friends. They had a very nice life.

Heidi Brauns taught six classes of gymnastics, each consisting of mixed ages and both sexes. She played volleyball and jogged, and she was the ping-pong champion of Clearwater. She ate everything she liked—cake, ice cream or whatever. She never slept more than four hours a night. She was five feet tall and weighed 122 pounds. She was seventy-eight.

She answered the door wearing a leotard with a

YMCA emblem, black net stockings, and slippers. For over two hours she never once sat down, nor did she ever stop talking, stop gesticulating, waving her arms, posing, demonstrating, quivering as though she were about to leap into the air. On the wall was a photograph of her doing a hand stand on parallel bars. It was taken fifty years ago. She could still do it.

She was upset about that awkward wire photo. That pose was intended for a side view. Look at the hands! The legs! When she made her first broad jump at four-teen, the instructor told her she had just broken the world's record. During the International Workers Olympics at Frankfurt-am-Main in 1925, she won four gold medals. She was thirty-one, but everyone assumed she was eighteen. She weighed ninety-eight pounds. When she came from Germany to the United States in 1929 and discovered all that cheap food, she stuffed her-self until she had gained twenty pounds. She never lost it. During World War I she had starved under the block-ade, living on two slices of plain bread a day and a few potatoes. She swore to herself that she would never again be hungry.

Her father and her husband were gymnasts, and so is her daughter, who once won five gold medals in one day at an AAU meet. She had some pictures of women in gym clothes in 1925. In the U.S. and in Germany they wore sailor blouses and dark blue knickers and bonnets, black stockings and belts. Heidi was a sensation. Black net stockings right up to her crotch! And no brassiere!

She quit school at fourteen and was teaching gymnas-tics at eighteen. World War I began a year later. She saw through the double standards, churches preaching "thou shalt not kill" and yet sanctifying war and victory. As the troop train transporting her brother waited at the station, she marched up and down, yelling at the soldiers:

"Why don't you go back? All of you. You want to be killed? For what? If you all stick together they can't send you off to war."

But the troops just looked at her, cowed, frightened, already wounded and dead. The year was 1914. She knew she would never have survived under Hitler.

After the war she was a union organizer and a political campaign worker. She married Karl, whom she met in a gym. She came to the U.S. in 1929, when she was thirty-four, and taught gymnastics in Brooklyn. They retired to Clearwater in 1961.

Heidi never really thought about old age until she was seventy, when she asked herself, "How old can I get?" She had always assumed that life began at forty or maybe it was fifty or sixty or whenever. She never got tired and still didn't feel any difference with age. Retirement kills. People should slow down but never stop working.

With her teaching fees and Social Security she was comfortable and could even save enough for occasional trips to Europe to visit her home town, where she was still a celebrity. She still didn't believe in God and found it impossible to believe in a life after death. The only true God was the goodness in the individual. People should have their religion within themselves.

"There is only one rule. All you have to do is love your neighbor like yourself."

She demonstrated the exercises she taught to middle-aged women. She did a few push-ups and knee bends and her imitations of animals. She jumped like a frog and waddled like a seal and walked like an elephant. But nevertheless the years were showing. She had liver blotches, and her skin was flabby under her arms. Her eyes had that thickened, cloudy look. Her breasts were shriveled, her body misshapen.

She went on with still another gym story, how she needed a monitor to restore her sense of confidence on the parallel bars after ten years without the proper equipment. But she did the trick perfectly. She was then seventy-three.

"The secret of life is to be calm all your life. And also work. But never retire. I am always amazed at what my body can do."

* * *

He was seventy-one. He parked his car and walked three blocks to a restaurant where he ate dinner. His car was black. It was a Galaxie and had an automatic transmission. After his meal he stepped outside, got into a car and drove home. He had some trouble with the transmission. It wouldn't shift. The next day a neighbor asked him about the new car in his driveway. Only then did he realize that he had driven home in a green Falcon with a straight shift. No charges were filed.

* * *

He was twenty-nine. With his arrival, greater Miami's population reached one million. He and his family were feted by the Chamber of Commerce, given gifts, publicity, celebrations, and plaques. Three months later he moved. It was too hot, too crowded, unfriendly, and humid. He didn't like his job. His wife couldn't stand the mosquitoes, the bugs, the three-inch flying cockroaches. Then he moved away from Phoenix, calling it a sandbox with mountains and 120-degree heat, depressed by the hordes of old people with asthma. But then he moved away from the Los Angeles area, saying the smog was unbearable. He is now forty. He lives in Connecticut. He loves it there. But when he retires he plans to move to Florida.

He was seventy-six. She was sixty-eight. He was riding his motorcycle up the avenue when she drove her car out of a side street and hit him. She was charged with failure to yield the right-of-way. He was in a hospital for a month. And then he died.

✳ ✳ ✳

5   The siren could be controlled three ways—by a button on the steering wheel, by a button on the floor, and by a manual switch. There were different positions on the manual control that produced three different sounds. The labels read *Yelp*, *Wail*, and *Hi-lo*. But on some of the rescue vans special effects could be produced by holding the switch between two clicks. And still others could be created by working the foot control and the manual at the same time.

It was an eerie music—demented bagpipes, a short-circuited synthesizer, banshees screeching through the sticky, hot night of Miami Beach. But more than anything else, it was the true voice of the victim, the cry of agony that alerted the city and disturbed its air-conditioned dream.

Sitting inside, clinging to the overhead grab rail, you could look through the window and see the reflections of that red and white dome light flashing from the roof, illuminating the hibiscus bushes and the palms, the rubber trees, the frangipani and the poincianas, throwing its quick, intermittent gleams against stucco walls and doors and through the windows of those hotels, rooming houses, efficiency apartments and retirement homes where a population was turning fitfully, sweating, aware of its infirmities, of its destiny, perhaps even wondering who it was being howled for out there in the night, who was having the traffic interrupted in his behalf, who was being granted the distinction of that blinding red/white signal, hi-loing, yelping, and wailing through the streets.

—red-WHITE-red-WHITE-red-WHITE—

Between runs you stood by at the station. Television sets were going. Telephones rang. Metal lockers opened and banged. Showers hissed. Industrious sounds came from the kitchen. Guys were coming upstairs from the volleyball court. The regular firemen were dressed in gray. Next to beds, lockers, desks or polished brass poles were their boots, with their empty bunker pants carefully rolled down over the tops. All the men had to do was shove their feet inside, reach down, yank up their pants and run.

But the others were wearing sky-blue jump suits with short black-leather boots. On the back it said FIRE RESCUE.

And it was between runs when you heard about the gory ones, the weird ones, the cases that went beyond the ordinary stroke and heart attack and pulmonary pneumonia and traffic injury. Like the old man who had been hit by a car while crossing the street. He had been wiped over the asphalt, leaving a painted streak of gore and blood that ended in a tangled heap of scattered brain and smashed arms and legs. The car didn't even stop. Or the guy who went off the roof of a condominium and landed in a soft flower bed, half burying himself in the ground. Or the old lady who had carefully climbed a ladder into a tree. It was late at night. Methodically, she broke away the twigs and small branches that got in her way. Then, very carefully, she hanged herself. The caretaker found her in the morning, wearing pajamas and a full-length mink coat, her eyes open, her tongue swollen and protruding and coated with a swarm of flies. At first he thought it was some kind of scarecrow.

A young, tanned, athletic man was slumped in a chair, his legs straight out, his eyes flickering back and forth to the television set and away again as he told you about the man who did a dive off the roof of a two-story house to land squarely on his head on the sidewalk. It split open like a rotten fruit, splattering its juices. When asked whose job it was to clean up the mess, he became confused. The question had never come up. His partner came in, picking his teeth. He didn't know either. The sanitation department, maybe. The fire department gets called out to hose down the street after a bad car accident to wash away the gas and oil. But not blood. Anyway. He shrugged. The ants would clean it all up fast enough.

The doctor told about one bizarre run they had recently made. They found an eighty-five-year-old man dead on arrival. He had been married four months. His wife was seventy-five. But it was a friend who had made the call to Rescue and had cleaned things up by the time they got there. He told them what had happened. The old man was giving it to his wife with a vibrator, but the

excitement was too much and his heart failed. He die
with the dildo clutched in his hand, still turned on.

A very young, good-looking fireman didn't ride rescu
anymore. He had become too depressed by the thou
sands of ailing, crippled, impoverished people who live
in Zone One, the South Beach area. He had been shocke
by the incidence of theft from the ill, the injured and th
dead. As they carried them off on stretchers, eager volur
teers would always hobble up to "take care of" thei
rings and watches. But during one run the good-lookin
kid discovered their $900 two-way radio was missing. A
eighty-year-old woman was running through the yar
and into an alley. He chased her around the building
into and out of her apartment and through the hallway
The radio was still giving coded emergency messages a
the wiry, stringy old lady tenaciously scurried away. B
the time he caught up with her and pried the radio ou
of her fingers, he was cursing and screaming. After
year of it he had to quit and go back to regular duty.

There was an old registered nurse who habituall
called the emergency medical service and then whe
they got there demanded they take her blood pressure
Another regular who complained of chronic pains in he
chest finally admitted she liked to hear the sirens. The
cured her by arriving silently. One woman was so fat sh
had to use a walker to move around. Her daughte
weighed about 200 pounds. She called the firemen to pic
her mother up and put her on the toilet. When one o
them made a remark about losing weight, she wrote
nasty letter to city hall. A woman fainted in front o
McDonald's hamburger stand. Her pulse was 130. Sh
was seventy-four. The rescue men revived her and tol
her to go to a hospital right away. She refused. An hour

ater they made another run. It was the same woman. She was dead when they arrived. They call it a signal 45.

Another woman told the rescue team when they arrived that she needed an enema. But she had the wrong guy. His nickname was the Animal, a Neanderthal redneck whose constant urge was to paint a Star of David on the side of the van every time they picked up a dead Jew. The Animal growled at her:

"The only way you'll get an enema out of me, lady, is if my toe squirts water when I kick you in the ass."

Station Two was headquarters. The Watch Office was the communications center that took all incoming calls, every message recorded on two very large reels of tape. Station Three was the country club, way up on 69th Street and Indian Creek Drive. It was a quiet area, big hotels and expensive homes. But condominiums were going up, the population increasing, traffic cases getting more common. Once a month the rescue men rotated their duty zones. They had to. Nobody could take more than a month of Zone One. It was referred to as the Pit or as Varicose Beach or as Shitsville.

Rescue Four was the back-up unit, a station wagon with a driver and the watch lieutenant. It had no doctor, but there was a stretcher, extra medical supplies, a suction unit, a cardiostat machine, a physiocontrol machine, a portable two-way radio, and a medical bag. A call came in: "Fourteen-sixty Ocean Drive. A woman down." The driver activated an ordinary siren, using a button on the steering wheel. He paused at every intersection, never taking the right-of-way for granted, never going at excessive speeds.

They arrived at one of those small, cheap hotels on the

ocean front. Rescue One was ahead of them. Lieutenant Morlock radioed in: "Rescue Four on the scene." Dr. Henriquez was already checking an old woman with a stethoscope as she sat on an aluminum chair on the front porch. There was a small puddle of vomit at her feet. She said she had emphysema and was having trouble breathing. They took her blood pressure and filled out a form. She said she was sixty-two. She looked much older. There wasn't much the doctor could do. Just as he was giving her a shot another call came in.

There was an accident on the causeway. An elderly-looking motorcyclist had had a blowout and spilled. His mouth was bleeding, and he had cuts and abrasions on his hands and arms. The police were already on the scene. The bike had a twisted fender, a broken headlight and windshield. They called for an ambulance "on a four," which meant no emergency, take your time. The man's wounds were bandaged. His arm was swelling rapidly, indicating a probable fracture. They put on a splint. The cop came over and knelt beside him, murmuring quietly. They were putting him under arrest. There was a warrant out on him for assault and battery. The motorcyclist didn't react, sitting quietly on the ground in his bandages. The rescue men picked up the dressing packages from the ground. A wrecker arrived.

Rescue Four decided to eat early in order to beat the rush. But just as they parked in front of the Miami Heart Institute a call came over the radio. "Sixteen-o-seven Michigan. Woman down." They got there the same time as Rescue One.

A group of very old people were sitting on the lawn on aluminum chairs. Others were standing around. The

patient was the fat old lady in the flower-pattern dress,
the one with the aggravated expression. She had a heart
condition. Every time she took her medicine she passed
out. They advised her to go to the hospital, but she didn't
want to go. There was always that conviction that once
you were in you would never come back. Not only that,
it cost $22.50 just for an ambulance. Medicare would pay
most of it, but . . . The woman was weak. Several neighbors helped her inside the very small, neat room filled
with furniture and mementos. She couldn't find the
right purse, the one with the Medicare card. One neighbor convinced her the records were already at the hospital. She had been there before. Her neighbor shoved two
crushed dollar bills into her hand.

Rescue Four went back to the Heart Institute and had
dinner in the cafeteria, the portable radio standing on
the table, a black obelisk, its polished antenna glistening,
alert and waiting. They talked about the weather. Because whenever it changed from hot to cold or from dry
to wet or the other way around, the number of runs
always increased sharply, mostly for pulmonary and respiratory problems. Miami Beach was the only city in
the United States with doctors actually riding in the
rescue vans. Before March 1972 each unit consisted of two
specially trained paramedics. At first there was a charge
when the doctor was added, but in October the city
decided to drop it. The service was now completely free,
including transportation to the hospital if the case was
critical. The rescue teams stood the traditional fireman's
watch—twenty-four hours on and forty-eight off.

Just as they finished coffee the radio alerted Rescue
One. "Two fifty-five Twenty-fourth Street. Mantell

Apartments. Woman stuck in elevator." On the way over there was another call in the same area. Rescue Two had to take it. The situation was already under control when Rescue Four got there. The old woman was out, sitting in the corridor in a wheelchair, suffering from broken ribs in a previous accident. But she had gone into a panic while trapped in the elevator, her pulse dropping to 40. She refused to go to the hospital.

Outside was a carnival of red and white flashing lights decorating the scene with eerie strobe effects. Rescue Two was working right across the street. An ambulance had also arrived. A man suffering from a stroke was being wheeled out of an efficiency-apartment building on a stretcher. His eyes were closed. His mouth was open.

They made another run back to 1460 Ocean Drive. It was the same woman, the one with emphysema. Rescue One was already there. One of the bystanders that afternoon had stolen her purse. Or perhaps it was "some girl." Her story rambled, her memory very poor. The police had called Rescue. The old woman had been staying at some sort of rest home, but they refused to take her back. Her clothes had disappeared. They couldn't take her to the hospital because she wasn't really sick. The Salvation Army agreed to take her for one or two nights.

She rode in the station wagon. At the city line they met with a black female Miami police officer who took the old lady off in her squad car. Lieutenant Morlock paused momentarily but then calmly got in front where the old lady had been sitting. On the way over she had vomited all over the seat.

10:59 P.M. The day room was dark. A fireman watching

Mutiny on the Bounty propped his stockinged feet up on a chair. His boots stood nearby, ready to run. Down in the Watch Office, the lights on the ready board were green, except for Rescue Three, which was yellow. The unit had gone off to get some ice cream for the firehouse. One of the lieutenants was saying they had made twenty-two runs that day. During the winter season that would go up to thirty. In 1971 they had a total of 10,373 emergencies.

11:45 P.M. The phone rang. A heart attack at the Lucerne Hotel. Room 715. 4101 Collins Avenue. There was a loud buzzer. A bell clanged twice. The dispatcher spoke over the p.a. system, his voice calm, dispassionate. Rescue Two came down the stairs, unplugged the equipment battery charger, slid the side door open and shut, roared out of the station and turned on the dome light, the siren used sparingly, whenever necessary, the driver careful, defensive, seeming almost slow. The unit arrived at 11:48. Three minutes. Carrying their equipment and their bags, the doctor and two paramedics took the elevator up and walked down the hall. They found a woman in bed in a nightgown, breathing with great difficulty, her face in pain. Her husband had already given her oxygen from a small, portable tank and a nitroglycerine tablet. They took her blood pressure. 230/106. She lay there panting, propped up by pillows, balding gray, old and shapeless, without teeth. Her eyes rolled around.

"They sure have nice-looking men in Florida."

"How long have you had high blood pressure?"

"Oh. A long time."

She was sixty-nine. They were from Bridgeport, Connecticut. She had been hospitalized recently, and there were ugly bruises on her thighs and calves from intravenous feedings. They smeared on electrolytic paste, preparing to take an EKG reading. The doctor listened with his stethoscope. A rescue man took her name, age and next of kin for his report. Her husband was nervous, wanting to help, not knowing how. He switched on lights and showed the doctor the many different pills his wife had been taking.

"She's been in and out of the hospital for eight months."

A paramedic adjusted the wrist straps and plugged in the EKG machine, the tape running out rapidly, scribbled with the inked messages transmitted by the woman's heart. The doctor gave her an injection in the shoulder as she turned her head and moaned, shutting her eyes. Her breathing was even more difficult, her potbelly sagging. They adjusted an oxygen mask on her face as the radio lying on the bed began crackling, alerting Rescue One to a possible heart attack. Dr. Comas scanned over the EKG tape. He pulled the strap of the woman's night dress off her shoulder and smeared paste on her chest underneath her small, shriveled breast. Quietly, he murmured, "Call an ambulance. On a three."

The message was relayed by radio. A suction-bulb recorder was attached to the woman's chest for another EKG reading. The doctor tried to give her an intravenous injection but had difficulty finding a vein. The woman moaned as he tried several times in the crook of the arm and then in the wrist. She moaned again. Her husband's face was impassive, but the pattern of his nervous movements revealed his anxiety. The doctor could not find a vein. He gave the woman another intramuscular injection instead.

The radio crackled with a message from Rescue One. A paramedic looked at the doctor and said, "They have a cardiac arrest." And then Rescue Four went out to help.

The doctor raised the woman's breast and moved the suction bulb. The radio crackled, "Bring the oxygen unit." Another EKG was taken. Dr. Comas moved to a lamp and ran the tape through his fingers. "Yes. It is the heart."

The radio was still busy. The woman moved, her face in agony, her chest rising and falling quickly. The report said, "Acute myocardial infarction."

Her husband was speaking to anyone at all: "I thought I brought her down here for recuperation."

The ambulance men arrived from Randle-Eastern. They moved the woman to the stretcher and strapped her in, taking the report and the EKG tapes. Rescue Two packed up its gear.

In the van they decided to go to Mt. Sinai and meet with Rescue Four when they came in with the cardiac arrest. They were ahead of the ambulance, running interference, stopping at an intersection with the light flashing, warning the traffic as the ambulance sped by. They parked by the emergency-room entrance and waited. The ambulance men unloaded the stretcher and wheeled their patient inside. A few seconds later one of the drivers came around the corner and yelled:

"She just arrested."

Rescue Two went inside, walking swiftly, passing a row of people sitting on chairs in the corridor, some sick, some waiting, all staring, bored, scared, impressed, and confused. They found the woman on a table in an emergency room. She was naked. Nurses, doctors, and interns scurried around the room, everyone yelling back and forth, speaking in abbreviations, slang, code, vernacular, medical terminology. Someone was shoving downward on her chest with the palms of both hands, using a hard, punching motion.. An EKG machine was running. Someone injected a needle into her chest, between her ribs and directly into her heart.

A man dressed in mixed whites and greens called out:

"She's got two beats, then one beat. Two beats, then one beat."

"Call respiratory therapy."

"Give her two amps of bicarb."

Someone was repeatedly trying to put a large, curved tube down her throat. He would pull it out, put his thumb in her mouth, raise her jaw, and put the tube in again.

Suddenly the swinging doors at the end of the corridor crashed open. It was Rescue One and Rescue Four, wheeling in a stretcher with a hugely fat, unconscious man strapped on it, naked except for a pair of boxer shorts. He was half bald and had a mustache. His face was blue and covered with vomit. A plastic tube hung out of his mouth. As they rolled him into Room 3, a nurse passed by and looked down, muttering with a cynical drawl, pronouncing her sentence with a rising and falling two-syllable stroke:

"He's dead."

It took eight men to move the patient onto a table. At first they tried to lift his body, and then they lifted the entire stretcher and slid him over. They pulled off his underwear. They cleared his throat with a suction machine and hooked him up to an EKG. One of the rescue men stood on a stool and whacked downward on the man's chest three times, paused and then three more. His pale-blue coveralls were dark with sweat. His eyes had a crazy look. He was lean and muscular and in top condition, and he was giving it all he had. He watched an oscilloscope monitor, the electronic ball bouncing all over the green vacuum tube as he massaged on the man's hairy, enormous chest. As he paused, he looked at the monitor. The signal passed across the tube in a perfectly straight line.

A doctor yelled out:

"No defibrillation? Shock him!"

Quickly, with expert, practiced movements, the interns and the nurses smeared his chest with two big gobs of white cream, holding two electric paddles on either side of his rib cage, two thick disks the size of a saucer fitted with vertical handles and wires. It was the Zapper. Everyone stood back. There was a warning to look out for the man's outstretched arms. They were ready. *ZAP!* Several thousand volts shot through the man's body which jumped spasmodically, his outstretched arms flying upward and then falling back.

The doctor gave him an injection into the heart and then with a roundhouse swing, he brought his fist down directly on the heart area. The crazy-eyed paramedic jumped up on the stool and began his massage again. One-two-three, pause. One-two-three, pause. The sweat was dripping off his cheeks and nose and chin, his uniform soaked. He stopped the massage as the doctor looked at the EKG tape.

"Straight line."

Crazy-Eyes started again. One-two-three, pause.
"Hold it."
Crazy-Eyes waited.
The doctor called out in a loud voice, like an auction-
eer, like the announcer at a bingo game:
"Straight line. Forget it. He's dead."
Everyone relaxed immediately and left the room.
Some men went to wash their hands at a large janitor's
sink at the end of the corridor. Others dabbed at the
vomit on their uniforms with paper towels. But Crazy-
Eyes wandered into Room 2, where the naked old
woman had once again gone into a cardiac arrest. He
jumped up on another stool and again began his frantic
massage. One-two-three, pause. One-two-three, pause.
Sweat dripping, muscles rippling, brows furrowed and
wrinkled, eyes bloodshot and flashing like the dome
lights on two speeding ambulances.

Others ran in to help. There were yells, questions,
instructions, numbers and readings.
"She's got three sodium bicarbs!"
Once again the woman began to recover, her heart
resuming its work. Dr. Comas said her chances of recov-
ery were now quite good. On the national average, only
one out of five people survives a heart attack. The rescue
teams save seven out of ten. Most of those who don't
make it die in the first four hours, 70 percent during the
first hour. He thought she would probably live another
six or seven years.

In Room 3 the dead man was alone. His face was a very
dark blue. There was no expression. His eyes were
closed. His arms flopped outward. His body was very
hairy, his ankles swollen, his toenails yellow, cracked,

and dirty. He was six feet five. He weighed about 400 pounds. He was forty-nine years old. The nurse closed the door.

Outside in the parking lot, Rescue One, Rescue Two, and Rescue Four were lighting up smokes, putting away their stretcher, cracking jokes. Follow up on any of their cases? No. Nobody cared that much. Lose one and win one. You can't get emotionally involved. It's just part of the job.

Lieutenant Morlock stood with his weight on one leg, smoking, covered with sweat. Crazy-Eyes danced a little jig, a quick shuffle, putting one hand on his hip and nudging the lieutenant as he arched his eyebrows and wriggled his buttocks.

"Thay, Thweetie. I didn't know thith wath your corner."

Lieutenant Morlock grinned.

Eleventh Street and Jefferson. Station One. The team had already made eleven runs in the eight hours they had been on duty. Their reports were on the desk.

"Subject complained of being unable to move her bowels." She was seventy-two. "Subject complained of being nauseated. Age eighty." "Subject was sleeping. Roomate said she complained of colon trouble. Age ninety-three." "Subject was lying on floor. Small cut on foot from broken glass tabletop. Belts tied together. Apparent suicide attempt. Moaning and screaming. Had apparently slipped out of noose. Age seventy-four." "Blood pressure 210/100. Abdominal pain. Age eighty-one." "Subject complained of pain in her chest. Age seventy-eight." "Subject took sleeping pill and didn't know it. Couldn't stay awake. Had thimble still on her finger as sleeping."

Dr. Gasteazoro was from Honduras. He was intelligent and charming and liked to talk. He had a private practice in Miami Beach but was trying to cut down his number of patients. He wasn't getting enough sleep. Frank, one of the paramedics, was a former lifeguard, tall and muscular, his hair long, his mustache in the fierce, medieval style of his northern Italian ancestors. Ray was quiet and unflappable, six foot five, his hair and mustache both conservative, a commercial fisherman and scuba diver. He and Frank went diving for crayfish together on their days off. As they stood around in the day room, the doctor smoked a small cigar and described a woman patient he once had who was worried about her ailment interfering with her sex life. It turned out she had sex every day. She was seventy-five. She wouldn't tell the doctor what her outlets were but insisted she got what she needed. Most women that age are incapable of sex. The vagina atrophies and gets very small. The lubrication glands dry up. The reproductive organs shrivel and cease to function.

7:01. Buzzer and bell. Voice on the p.a.: "Three-fifty Ocean Avenue. Lord Balfour Hotel. Possible heart attack." Frank muttered as they went outside to the van, "That's the second time today. Same address."

They arrived in a little over one minute. A small, thin Jewish man sat on a sofa in the lobby, a single crutch by his side. He was in pain, his breathing shallow. He was seventy-two. Frank got the stretcher as Ray took his blood pressure. 120/70. Very good. But his neck veins were engorged. It still looked like a cardiac. The man moaned. He didn't want to go to the hospital.

"I just came back from there."

Very quietly the doctor spoke to him:

"If you don't go to the hospital, you're going to die. I can't tell you any plainer than that."

It took the help of another old man to persuade him. With great reluctance he got on the stretcher and allowed himself to be strapped in with his crutch and covered with a blanket. With lights and siren, they went to the South Shore Hospital, arriving nine minutes after getting the call. The man moaned and gasped, struggling when the doctor tried to give him an injection.

As he was wheeled into the emergency room he complained of sweating although he wasn't. He seemed terrified and started to vomit, moaning as an IV needle was inserted. "You're breaking my *arm.*" His clothes were removed. They prepared him for an EKG, took a blood sample and gave him five mg.s of morphine. He grew pale and suddenly calm, accepting the ministrations of the intern, a Cuban nurse and a Chinese resident. His heartbeat was shown on the monitor. You could see the PVCs, the premature ventricular contractions. If these misfires should happen to fall on top of a T-wave, it could cause a fibrillation. This is a major backfiring of the heart. It becomes confused and disorganized. Instead of beating, it lies dormant, quivering. Unless it can be set in motion again, the patient dies.

Rescue One left the ER. They went upstairs to the intensive-care unit to visit a man they had picked up on their last shift, three days before. But he was sleeping under heavy sedation, wearing an oxygen mask. He was seventy-five and looked terrible, but Frank was very proud of him. When they got the call he was already "dead" from a cardiac arrest, and they had nearly given him up. They had even broken three of his ribs while giving him heart massage.

At 7:35 they were O-9, back in service. But instead of returning to quarters, Rescue One stopped off at the Causeway Marina to visit with some old fishing buddies who sat at a table on the dock by the bay, drinking booze and telling stories. At 8:13 an amiable drunk was telling about his World War II flying days and the incident of the frozen parachute. The radio crackled. "Woman down." Rescue One arrived in three minutes. A woman had stumbled on the sidewalk, had fallen into a hedge and couldn't get up. She had been there a half hour. People were watching from windows, from the patios of rooming houses and residential hotels. Finally, someone had called.

The victim had heard a woman on the sidewalk saying: "Morris. Leave her alone. Don't get involved."

There was no apparent problem. She was a little confused. She probably suffered from a vascular insufficiency, the general debility and senility of old age. She wouldn't say how old she was but appeared well into her seventies. Rescue One gave her a lift. As soon as she sat in the van she wiggled her hips, squirming against the doctor.

"Ohhh. You like to play. I like to play too. All these handsome men. They could give me just what I need."

It was an unusually quiet night. Melvyn Douglas was starring in *Ghost Story* on TV. He was a warlock who contrived the death of an old family domestic. The firemen, the doctor, and the paramedics were engrossed. Over the radio in the next room you could hear a message to another unit—"Man passed out . . ." The rest of the words were overwhelmed by the eerie, dramatic theme music. At 10:00 they watched *Banyon*.

At 10:30 they made a run to 1535 Jefferson, arriving at 10:32. A seventy-seven-year-old man had "a pain in the stomach." He was unable to get his own doctor. The pain was in the gall-bladder area. He had had previous heart attacks and had already taken two nitroglycerines. Frank radioed for an ambulance on a three as Ray took the man's blood pressure. The doctor was irritated. It was difficult to determine whether or not the man had ever had gall-bladder trouble before. There was a collection of pills on the table. When Frank asked the man for his next of kin he got a wise-guy answer and then, "None." Then he tried to change it, but Frank refused to make a change. They began to exchange gentle insults and threats, interrupted by Ray's and Frank's admiration of a left-handed fishing reel on the kitchen table.

"You like it? Keep it."

"Are you serious?"

"Yeah. Sure."

The ambulance arrived. Very cheerfully, the man got on the stretcher. They wheeled him out. At 10:45 they were watching the rest of *Banyon*.

It was quiet for nearly two hours. The fire lieutenant was a tough, scarred old-timer, very proud of his engines and ladder, one of which was a classic 1943 Pirsch, another a big, new, gleaming American La France. It was hot outside, with the mugginess of the tail end of the hurricane season. Station One was directly under the takeoff pattern of Miami International Airport, the jets thundering upward, passing overhead and then out to sea to make their turns and set their courses north. The streets were silent. Nothing moved.

12:51. "Royal Hotel. Seven fifty-eight Washington Avenue. Woman with a broken arm." Rescue One was asleep. Within seconds they were out of their bunks, into their short boots and in the van. In the lobby of the hotel a drunken woman was sitting on the floor in the middle of the scattered debris of an ashtray. One arm was in an Ace bandage, a loose, dirty sling dangling around her neck. She was crying in a slurred, maudlin way.

"I'm a tough GI."

Another woman puffed nervously on a cigarette, her breath smelling of alcohol. She kept insisting that the drunk's shoulder was broken in two places. Helped to her feet, the subject refused to sit in a chair and submit to an examination. She staggered in a small, helpless circle, complaining that her arm hurt. Then she insisted on going upstairs. Ray and Frank took her up in the tiny elevator. The doctor remained in the lobby. Ray was quiet and patient. Frank argued and taunted her.

"I was in the Third Air Force and I'm pretty tough."

"Yeah. Sure. What are you? Irish?"

"I'm French and German. And I'm a nurse, too."

She staggered around in the hall, refusing to go into her room. Ray finally persuaded her. As she unlocked the door she turned coy.

"Please excuse me. My room is a mess."

Ray got her to lie down as Frank stayed out in the hall and laughed at her. They closed the door and left. Down in the lobby the other woman had been joined by a third. They smoked rapidly, muttering, "She won't stay."

Frank growled on the way out, "Next time, don't call us. Call the cops."

There were no more runs that night. Ray told about the time he and Frank responded to the call "Car in the water." They donned their scuba gear and went in with a splash. Down. Down. Finding no one inside, they searched the nearby bottom. Later they found out that the car had been reported and checked earlier that morning.

The next team was quiet and talked very little. The doctor's name was Bencomo, but one of the rescue men, a licensed practical nurse who worked at Mt. Sinai on his days off, was always referred to as The Doctor.

3:26: "Woman limp and unresponsive." But it was really a signal 35. She was drunk. At 4:20 they went to 950 Pennsylvania Avenue. "Woman down on floor. People can't get in." As they parked, two old ladies walked by on the sidewalk. One of them was saying:

"She's gone with the wind. She's dead as a doornail. How they gonna get in?"

Inside the building an old woman was crying. She hadn't seen her all day. They would have to break down the door. But although the double doors were flimsy, there were no tools. A city policeman stood by. The maintenance man came up with a cheap screwdriver. He tried to pry open the outer door, but the screwdriver bent in the middle. With his pliers, he removed the pin from the top hinge but couldn't get the bottom one out. Several men took turns kicking at the door. The locks finally gave.

The woman was in the kitchen, slumped down in a

corner. She was still breathing. When they dragged her out into the middle of the floor, she moved ever so slightly. Dr. Bencomo said, "Stroke." They gave her oxygen and called an ambulance on a three. She breathed more deeply. Her face became bright red. She began to quiver, her left leg and foot shaking. The driver showed Dr. Bencomo a can of dietetic salmon. Perhaps she was a diabetic. Her blood pressure was 130/70. Pulse 76. She was breathing well, her life signs good. The driver found two pill bottles. They were for high blood pressure.

Someone went to find the manager to be a witness to the door damage. The old woman who had been crying discovered then she had a spare key to the room. She was so upset she hadn't thought about it. The ambulance arrived with the same attendants who had made the last run. Rescue One went to a municipal garage and tanked up with gas. Dr. Bencomo said the woman might or might not recover. There was no way to predict when she would regain consciousness—if ever. And there was no way of predicting the extent of the permanent brain damage.

Back in quarters. There was a book in the day room. It was about the positive and negative impulses of the heart, about P-waves and R-waves and T-waves, about QRS cycles, arrhythmia and atrial fibrillations.

"Ten fifty-one Collins. A sick man." One of the beachfront hotels. Arrive in two minutes. Up the stairs. A mezuzah fastened to the door with electrician's tape. There were plastic flowers standing in vases on a bureau and on the window sill. There were some very cheap reproductions of paintings on the wall, a Jewish calendar and a picture of a young man with a handlebar mustache standing in an ancient uniform. It was the subject himself as an officer in the Rumanian Army ten years or so before World War I.

The man was dizzy. That very day he had seen a doctor, who had given him some pills. He had not eaten. But he had vomited anyway. His wife was crying. He was fat and he was ninety years old. On a bureau was a recent photograph of a beautiful boy and girl. There were other pictures of his children and grandchildren. His blood pressure was very low. The Doctor radioed for an ambulance on a four. Dr. Bencomo asked for all the man's pills and medications and then decided to cancel the ambulance. Rescue One would transport the patient.

At 5:27 a woman lay on her couch with chest pains. Her husband had broken a leg a few weeks before. He had a cast and a cane. He was a little nervous but not much, saying nothing at all to his wife. Two neighbor women came in, awed and very worried. The subject was seventy. She was given oxygen and an injection. She moaned that she felt much better. There were amateur paintings on the walls, a TV set, gewgaws, pictures of young children, old photographs of the husband and wife. An ambulance team showed up. Rescue One disconnected its oxygen and packed up. The Doctor said, "Momma. Next time you shouldn't wait so long."

Back to the station, the day room, the book. Read about wandering pacemakers, extra beats and skips, rates, infarctions, bradycardia, PVCs, sinus arrest, ... (The radio was saying, "Rescue Three . . . behind hotel . . . man in the water calling for help . . .") . . . atrial flutter, Wenckebach phenomenon . . .

5:49. The phone rang. They were cleared for a twelve

and went to the Turf Pub for dinner. Everyone was depressed. There was no conversation. The radio stood between a soup bowl, a bread basket and a butter dish, hoarsely prattling something about Engine Three and about a boat in distress. They returned to the station and watched *Zulu* on TV.

7:36. 900 West Avenue. Apartment 833. Man having a heart attack. On the way over, the motor stalled. It took several tries to get it started again. High-rise condominium. Elevator. Man on sofa, mouth open, sweating, felt cold, age seventy-four, white hair, listless, very dizzy, no longer had original pains in chest, had fallen down several times last week. BP 110/70. The furniture was Sears/fancy. The subject was given oxygen.

"I don't want to go to the hospital."

"Sam. Why take a chance? I don't think I could take it again. Sam. Please."

"I don't wanna go. I'm tired. I wanna go to bed."

"But that's what's *wrong* with you."

An ambulance was called. An EKG test was taken in an effort to convince the patient that it was an emergency. Outside in the bay, a large sightseeing boat was going by. Group singing could be heard approaching over the water, the toot of a whistle, the ring of a bell, a cheerful tour-guide voice over a p.a. system. "Hello *dere!*" Applause. Whistles. Cheers. A crowd of elderly residents stood in the patio by the pool, laughing and yelling back at the boat. The Miami skyline was visible through the apartment window as Rescue One fastened the straps over the dabs of paste. The subject's wife called the answering service and asked to speak to their doctor. The EKG was normal, but this could still be a case of serious insufficiency.

"Oh, gee. They never do anything at night. I've been there . . . so many times."

The subject moaned, tired, frustrated, hopeless. But when the ambulance arrived, he agreed to go.

Back at the station, the British soldiers were still firing at the Zulu warriors.

8:08. False alarm. Headquarters pushed the wrong button. Rescue Three was wanted. A bus driver had been beaten up and robbed.

8:20. 825 Washington Avenue. Apartment 218. Clinton Hotel. Man fell down and couldn't get up. A crowd of old people were gathered around the TV in the lobby watching *All in the Family*. Archie Bunker was sounding off as the rescue men squeezed into the elevator. It was a cramped, ratty apartment. There were two narrow beds. The man was lying on his back on the bathroom floor. The woman was small, old, weak, and nervous. The men picked up the patient and put him back in bed. He was eighty-two. He used a walker, but sometimes he could stand up by himself. He was completely bald, his voice very weak and hoarse. His wife didn't understand the question when The Doctor asked for their name until he said:

"Vas iz de Namen?"

8:32. The Zulus were making their final charge on the fort. Fire swept through the barracks. There were spears, rifles, war chants, death. The day room was crowded with watching firemen.

10:27. A Cuban woman called the police to report a burglary. When the detective arrived he found her passed out and called Fire Rescue. Dr. Bencomo talked to her in Spanish. He patted her face. They took her blood pressure. A younger sister said she had a history of heart trouble. There was little response and then a moan. She woke up, crying and gasping, very short of breath and unable to talk. A detective began to dust various objects for fingerprints, using a very fine brush and powder, working with methodical, slow concentration. There was a Catholic icon on the wall, a statuette of the Madonna, the red/white flasher reflecting on its features through the open door.

The woman gasped and choked and then suddenly rolled over in another dead faint. An ambulance was called on a three. Her brother came home from work, his face, hands and arms streaked with grime. He was cool. Earlier in the evening he had seen three suspicious guys in front of the house and followed them up to 20th Street. He had their tag number and gave it to the cops. He had been suspicious because their apartment had already been robbed three weeks earlier.

The woman recovered consciousness and began crying. The ambulance arrived. Rescue One went back to the station to watch the late news. Three black extremists had hijacked a jet and demanded ten million dollars' ransom for the return of their hostages. The FBI had shot out the plane's tires as it took off from Orlando. The plane was then circling Key Biscayne, just a few miles away from Miami Beach. The hijackers demanded to speak to President Nixon over the radio. He refused.

Monday. Ray and Frank and Dr. Gasteazoro were back on duty. They got a call for a "woman sick." But her doctor had told her relative to get an ambulance and send her to Mt. Sinai. The relative thought you first had to call Fire Rescue to get an ambulance.

Back at Station One. Stan Gordon, the Philosopher, was a well-read, thoughtful fireman who had ridden rescue in 1966 when it first started. He told the story of the great showboat act he had once put on when he found a dead man on a bus right in front of city hall. He was good and dead. Really dead. But the Philosopher went through the whole number: mouth-to-mouth resuscitation, heart massage, blood pressure, pulse. A doctor arrived from somewhere, took one look, gave the Philosopher a certain smile, and joined the act. There was a large crowd. Rescue was a new concept then. They lacked money and equipment, there was political resistance, and everyone was conscious of the public image. So it was true street theater. The doctor gave an IM injection, IV solutions, and listened with his stethoscope. But there was nothing to hear except the moans and mutters of the sidewalk audience.

The Philosopher also told several stories of finding bodies that had been dead for days in locked apartments. You could always recognize that smell even as you were going up the stairs. Once they had a new man. They had just finished a big spaghetti dinner. Catching that familiar odor, they talked him into going up to check out the problem, laughing hysterically when he threw up all over the hall.

Rescue One got restless and went for a ride to the beach. At the jetty they checked out the girls and then went down to the Chamber of Commerce fishing docks. Ray carried the radio in the back pocket of his coveralls.

There was a call to treat an epileptic at the city jail. They went in through the back door, but no guards were around. Everyone was confused. It seemed the prisoner was an habitual drunk, a revolving-door case. They only wanted an ambulance, but everybody thought they had to call Rescue first. Ray and Frank went to the front desk to get that matter settled once and for all. But there was a hassle, a buck-passing contest, and finally they went to lunch at a sandwich shop.

At 4:58 there was a possible stroke. The man was eighty-six, unable to talk, his mouth quivering, a wet cloth on his forehead, his right facial muscles twitching. It was motor aphasia. The man wanted to talk but couldn't. He had paresis of the right side. His wife was quite deaf. She fumbled through a pack of doctors' business cards. A neighbor was running the show, yelling at her, giving instructions, two other neighbors joining the chorus, trying to make the woman understand about getting his Medicare number. The radio was saying something about Engine One and a stuck elevator. There were porcelain gewgaws everywhere, cheap furniture, doilies on the arms and back of the sofa, plastic flowers, and two very large, framed portraits of the man and the woman in dignified poses, rendered in oils in 1929.

At 5:50 they were at the Causeway Marina. There was wine, jokes, laughter, fishing stories, handshakes. A call came in. "Lincoln Road and Pennsylvania. Man down." They found him lying in a flower bed on the mall. A police car was there and a crowd. The man was hemorrhaging at the mouth. Witnesses said he had a cramp in his leg, sat down and started shaking. He wore a hearing aid. His mouth kept moving, but he was unconscious. Rescue One put him on a stretcher, gave him oxygen and transported him to South Shore Hospital. At the ER he was hooked up to the EKG monitor, which showed some PVCs and some arrhythmia. His pressure was good. His

tongue had been bitten, which meant possible convul-
sions, perhaps epilepsy. The subject was catheterized.
An IV was started. He was given several shots. Two
doctors at once listened with stethoscopes. Nobody
knew his name, and they went through his wallet looking for identification. The man started to struggle. He
had to be held down to get a needle in his vein.

Two ambulance drivers came in, and they started jok-
ing around with Ray and Frank. They left at 6:10 and
went back to the Causeway Marina.

6:25. 1000 West Avenue. It was a very fancy apartment
house, the lobby floors of white marble, bas reliefs on the
walls. Inside the apartment a woman was sitting on the
sofa. There was a moment of confusion. The older
woman at the door just looked.

"I didn't think there would be so many of you."

"Where's the patient? What's the trouble?"

"She's sick. You know what I mean?"

And then the woman on the sofa started screaming.
"NO! *NOOO!*"

"I called her doctor and he said to get an ambulance.
Why are there so many? Four men? There used to be
two. I know. My brother-in-law lives upstairs and he's a
regular customer. Is this the usual thing to have so
many? This will upset her. Oh, Doctor. What do you
think I should do?"

"Madam. I am not a psychiatrist. I can only suggest
you do as her doctor ordered."

"Oh. What can I do? I'm all alone. There's nobody to
tell me what to do."

The mother paced very rapidly and very nervously,
her fingers at her mouth twitching, folding and unfold-

ing. Her daughter was thirty-eight, her face in a grimace of frustration and anxiety. She watched her mother. Curious but cringing, she looked at those four men, three with mustaches and tans, hair and muscle, all six feet and over, the fourth one wearing a long white coat.

"NO! NO! *NOOOOOOO!*"

"Oh. I'm all alone. Look. Supper all ready. And she didn't eat a morsel."

"*NO!*"

The mother clutched at her daughter's shoulder, yelling into her face.

"What's *wrong* with you? How do you *feel?*"

The daughter ran into the other room. Dr. Gasteazoro stayed, smoking his cigar. Ray radioed for an ambulance. Frank pleaded with them to let him handle it. He knew he was good at this. He had experience. He had the feel for it. They waited. Frank's voice was murmuring quietly in the other room, rapidly, comforting, soothing. The woman's mother kept trying to interfere. Ray kept trying to convince her to stay out.

"What's he doing to her? That's all I want to know. Is he giving her medicine or what? An injection? She was all right until so many of you came in. She's terrified of crowds. There used to be only two. Wasn't there only two? Oh. What shall I *do?* I'm all alone."

The ambulance arrived with a stretcher. Frank brought the woman out, murmuring to her softly, his arm loosely and gently around her shoulders. She was sobbing and shaking, frightened of the six men who surrounded her, one of them holding a black, secret radio, another writing things down on a big clipboard.

As Rescue One walked out of the lobby, an old woman

approached, smiling with the assurance of knowing that it was obviously not her number that was up.

"What? You're leaving with no patient? That's good. Ha?"

Just as they pulled away, they got another call. 1498 Jefferson, a cheaper building but brand new. The man was fifty-four. He was half bald, quite fat, with no muscles at all. He suffered from chronic emphysema, but this was his worst attack. He was clammy and cold and had already used his own oxygen twice that day. But then his foot turned blue and he got a pain around his heart. The television was on as he and his wife gave the doctor his medical history. The room was immaculate, thoroughly air-conditioned, the furniture cheap/new and all neutral tans and whites. The wife noticed the TV and turned it off.

The elevator was too small for a stretcher. The patient sat on a chair with his arms crossed over his chest, trembling and weak and very frightened. Frank grabbed the legs and Ray held the back, carrying the man out. Outside the apartment a woman of about ninety passed in the hall.

"What's going on in there?"

Dr. Gasteazoro replied, "Lady, that's none of your business."

"Oh. So you're a nasty sonofa bitch. Huh?"

It was difficult getting everyone in the elevator. And then the patient's face turned blue. The oxygen carrying case had to be opened, the mask pulled out and applied, the valve turned on. The elevator stopped at another floor. The door opened. An old woman shrank back at the scene inside.

Getting out was even more complicated, the door opening and closing and banging against shoulders and legs. The stretcher was taken out of the van, the patient shifted, the chair returned. As the van pulled away with its light flashing and the siren yelping, a terrified cat ran in front of it and was almost killed.

At the emergency room, the man from the flower bed was stabilized and comfortable. He could talk, complaining of being cold even though he was under a thick blanket. The emphysema patient was given shots and oxygen and IVs. A needle was stuck into his groin to draw blood from the femoral vein to test for gas content.

Rescue One left at 7:05. Twenty minutes later they made another run to 1500 Bay Road, the Morton Towers. There were trickling garden pools, a huge lobby, a milling crowd of gawking people. The apartment was quite large. Six elderly well-dressed people had been spending the evening watching TV after dinner when suddenly one of them started to stare blankly. He was fully conscious but didn't talk or respond or move. He was eighty-three. Blood pressure 190/105. The doctor picked up the man's left arm and let it go. It fell slowly. The right arm fell hard. Occasionally the man stopped breathing. In a moment he resumed. It was the Cheyne-Stokes syndrome. The doctor muttered, "Right paresis."

Three more elderly people came in, cautious, quiet, in awe. The man's wife was dead. His sister was his next of kin. The ambulance crew arrived, the same ones who had just returned from Jackson Memorial Hospital where they had taken the psychotic woman. There were many jokes and wisecracks. They moved the stroke victim to the stretcher leisurely, pausing to talk with the

escue men, laughing about that kooky mother who had
iven them a bad time all the way to Miami. Besides.
'hat girl didn't need a psychiatrist. All she needed was
 hot beef injection.

At 8:57 they were eating dinner, a very special *paella*
nade of chicken and rice that Rescue One had bought
hat afternoon at the Publix market, but also of clams
nd fish and lobsters that Ray and Frank had caught
hemselves. They were eating it gingerly, waiting for it
o cool, shooting the bull with a fire captain and a lieu-
enant and the Philosopher about the Russian bottled-
;as deal and about Wankel rotary engines and about
ome of the famous rescue runs of the past. And then
:ame the buzzer, the bell and the p.a. system. "Fourteen
wenty-three Collins. Woman fell out of bed. Fainted.
Iusband and manager put back in bed. Bleeding." They
an through the kitchen and down the hall, following
ine another down the brass sliding pole.

They arrived. The lobby was full of old people, all
vatching the same TV program. The elevator was tiny.
The woman upstairs was in bed, moaning with small
inimal sounds of distress. Her face was a bright blue, and
;he was given forced oxygen immediately. Her husband
vas a small man, very nervous, sweating, frightened. He
:ept asking if he should close the window until Dr. Gas-
eazoro said yes, sure. Go ahead and close the window.
They would have to carry her down on a chair. She was
hrashing and yet limp as they laid her on the floor and
;ot a hard chair under her, keeping the oxygen on her
ace. But the elevator was so small everyone couldn't fit
n. The husband and the doctor ran down the stairs,
:arrying the oxygen. The woman was moaning,

"Momma . . . momma . . . momma . . . momma . . ." As she was carried through the lobby, the old, wrinkled faces with the white hair and the suntans turned away from the TV to stare with stunned expressions.

Rescue One moved very fast. She was strapped to the stretcher, lifted in and locked in place. Her husband got in the back with her. The red/white flashed. The siren yelped and wailed. The husband was very agitated, almost sobbing, trying to touch her arm, to stroke her face. "Rose, Rose. I'm *here.*" He repeated the story of his wife's fall and nose-bleed and the scratch on her leg. She was sixty-eight. Or sixty-five. He wasn't sure. They had just come down from New York.

South Shore Hospital. Push through the double doors and roll down the corridor and into the ER. The husband was told to stay outside. The woman moaned for her mother. Again, she turned cyanotic blue. She was put in bed, her nightgown cut away with scissors. She was given oxygen. She had no pulse. The p.a. system called for the respiratory therapist, but he wasn't available. Neither were the emergency-room doctors. Two cardiac arrests were occuring at the same time somewhere upstairs. Dr. Gasteazoro helped out during the emergency.

In the next bed the old man with the stroke from their previous run was looking around, conscious but not moving; a neurologist poking his hand with a pair of scissors. There was no reaction at all. But his eyes were busily watching the activity around the bed next to him.

The woman's heart stopped and then started. There was a frantic scurry of movement, the doctor, the nurse and an intern speaking rapidly, giving injections, heart massage, adjusting machines. The doctor tried to get an endotracheal tube down her throat, but the woman was fighting him and there was some sort of obstruction. He couldn't get it in. There was a desperate struggle. Dr. Gasteazoro bent down and blew on the end of the tube by mouth. There was a loud gurgle in her stomach. No good. He pulled the tube out and tried it again, stopping to put the oxygen mask over her face, although this wasn't really getting any air into her lungs. The EKG monitor was showing one premature ventricular contraction after another. Her heart was misfiring very badly. Another tube, another try, pry up the jaw, turn her head back, shove it into her mouth and down her throat. Again the air went into her stomach.

Her toes were deformed. She had horrible bunions and wore pink polish on her toenails. Staring down at her nude body, her fat stomach distended by air, you had to wonder just how many dreary, plodding miles those feet had traveled. The nurse and the paramedics exchanged looks. She was going. The doctor got the tube in and hooked up the oxygen breathing machine, but he wasn't sure if it was going into the stomach or the lungs. He put his stethoscope on her belly and listened. He disconnected the breathing machine and pulled the tube out. The woman vomited.

The intern gave it a try with another tube. The ambulance drivers came in, kidding around with giggles and jokes and fag routines. "Say. This one's kind of cute." The monitor was going crazy, the electronic ball bouncing every which way. But the rate itself was slowing. They were still struggling with the endotracheal tube. And then. Finally. Into the lung. Quickly they connected the breathing machine. The doctor gave her heart massage—one-two-three. The rate on the monitor began to increase. But then it slowed. There were some PVCs. Frank took over the heart massage. One-two-three. There was a gasp from the breathing machine. One-two-three. *Gasp.* Everyone looked at the monitor and watched the patterns. Only then did the nurse pull the curtain part way across to partially shield the view of the stroke victim, whose only response was with his eyes and with his left hand, nervously fidgeting with the top of the sheet.

The woman's face was blue and purple. Her eyes were half open. Tubes were in her mouth and in her nose, her expression grotesque. There was some heart movement on the monitor. Someone said, "Hell. She might make it." Everyone smiled. It was a joke. Frank did it again. One-two-three. *Gasp.* A PVC. Another PVC. Pause and another PVC. Dr. Gasteazoro checked her pupils. *Gasp.* He pushed down on her stomach, which caused a tremendous burp. There were giggles, snickers and smiles around the room. A few people came into the ER, technicians or interns. Eleven people were around the bed. But she had no pulse. The nurse felt around the femoral vein and said she thought she felt something. One of the ambulance boys said, "What you feel in there is a worm eating her from the inside."

"There's nothing. No cerebral. I guess we'll have to let her go." The doctor pulled the tube away from the oxygen. He listened to her heart with a stethoscope. "No pulse. But there's still a heart sound."

He put the oxygen back. Someone mentioned the husband outside. They said he was nervous and about to

)llapse. There were jokes about putting him in the next
ed. They gave the woman a shot of sodium bicarbonate.
rank pumped on her chest—one-two-three. And then
ie doctor called out, "Ventricular fibrillation. Get out
ie Zapper."

Everyone stood back. The cream, the paddles—*ZAP!*
They gave her one shot. And then they quit. Everything
·as turned off. She had gone over six minutes without
ir. More than three minutes causes brain damage. Even
ˉ she lived now she would be a vegetable. The air was
:opped. The doctor listened with his stethoscope. Ever-
one watched the monitor. The rate decreased. The
·VCs were very slow.

There was something very shiny on the woman's left
nee, something sparkling against the blue of her skin.
t looked like a diamond. An ambulance guy reached
own and picked at it. It was a sequin. Somehow it had
ome off a dress or a slipper or a purse. She must have
nelt on it, and it had become imbedded in her skin,
·erhaps during her first fall in the hotel room.

"Listen. Did she breathe just then? This is ridiculous."

Snickers. Snorts. Quickly, the doctor hooked the air
·ack on. Frank gave her more heart massage. One-two-
hree. Everyone gazed in silence at the electronic signal.
ind then again, they gave up.

There were jokes about orange juice and cheesecake.
)ne ambulance guy goosed the other. "Say, honey. Puh-
eeze."

People left the ER. Others stayed, watching the moni-
or. The pattern changed, the rate slower and slower.
The stroke victim's eyes were trying to see what was
;oing on. No one noticed him. The electronic signal

wobbled, wavered, jerked, forming a shapeless, spasmodic pattern.

The woman was already dead, but the exact moment of legal death was arbitrary. Her brain had gone a long time before. But her heart could keep on beating for possibly another hour, quivering, spastic, making meaningless motions. At 10:08 Rescue One left the ER, turning for one last look at the monitor.

The woman's husband was still outside in the corridor, pale, pacing nervously back and forth, alone. No one said anything to him. They put the stretcher back in the van and returned to quarters. On the way back, the doctor was quiet and thoughtful. The woman would have lived if he had been able to get that tube down her throat. Perhaps it was a congenital deformity. Perhaps a swollen larynx.

Both of the cardiac arrests upstairs had also died.

The *paella* was ruined. It was stale and overcooked and sticky. They picked at it, then threw it away, washing the dishes.

10:50. Another run. 405 Espanola Way. A "sick man." It was a ratty hotel, an alcoholics' dive, everything brown, faded, stained. The manager let them into Room 205, saying the maid could not get in that morning. They found the man naked, lying on his back, sprawled in an easy position. He had been dead at least five hours, perhaps twelve. The doctor pointed to the discoloration on the bottom side of his limbs and body. He also pointed to the swelling in the man's groin about the size of a baseball.

"Not only is he dead. He also has a hernia."

There was an empty fifth on the floor, lying on its side.

There was an empty pint of Old Taylor. There was another fifth, not quite empty. There was vomit in the bottom of the wastebasket. The man was lean and he wore a neat mustache. Rescue One sat in wicker chairs on the sidewalk and waited until a policeman came. An old man came hobbling up and started to gossip. He said the dead man had worked at Wolfie's on 17th Street. The cop arrived at 11:05.

On the way back they drove to a Cuban restaurant where Dr. Gasteazoro bought himself a cigar. He smoked it with little satisfaction, preoccupied and subdued, pondering, unsettled. As they passed Dipper Dan's, Ray stopped the van. The door was locked, but the guy inside opened it for them. They all ordered ice-cream cones. And you had a double chocolate.

*　*　*

He was sixty-three. He was blind. Without realizing it, he was wearing his drinking buddy's hat. He refused to give it up, and when his buddy grabbed his cane and beat him over the head with it twelve times, he pulled a pistol out of his pocket and fired three shots. He missed. Charges of carrying a concealed weapon were dismissed on the grounds of self-defense. His drinking buddy was fifty-seven. Charged with larceny of his own hat and assault with a deadly weapon, he spent a month in jail before the case was heard and dismissed. The men are still close friends.

*　*　*

He was eighty-four. He rode a bicycle and sold old clothes to the blacks. His house was filled with piles of rags, closets full of rags, bags full of rags. He had no electricity, no running water, no telephone, no gas. The carpets, the paintings, the baby grand were all covered with litter and dust. The TV was unplugged.

The Chrysler with 5,000 miles had been up on blocks for fourteen years. He took showers naked in the driveway when it rained. He ate no meat. He collected old vegetables thrown away by the supermarkets. The neighbors complained. He was warned, arrested, and then committed to an institution as mentally incompetent. A year later some kids set fire to the house. The firemen found $15,630 in undamaged cash in a closet. They found $17,630 in scorched but spendable currency, $2,506 in badly damaged currency, $1,385.52 in coins, several bank books, six rings, four watches, a diamond brooch and necklace and stock certificates worth $850. It was discovered he had over $50,000 in banks. By court order he had to pay $569 per month to the nursing home. He also had to pay $504 per week for a twenty-four-hour guard to protect the house he was not allowed to live in. But the Internal Revenue Service froze his assets. He had paid no income taxes for six years.

Eleven years ago his sister was sick. He didn't believe in doctors. For three days she sat up in bed, unable to sleep, recognizing no one. His best friend helped him give her an enema. It worked. She went to sleep immediately. A half hour later she was dead. She was sixty.

His house has now been condemned and bulldozed to the ground, the property sold. By court order, all his personal possessions were sold at a public auction. His lawyer paid his bills, including $5.32 to the Florida Power and Light Company and $10,987.97 to the Internal Revenue Service. But then the IRS demanded another $3,042.25 for interest. He is still at the nursing home. He has had no visitors.

6   There are those sliding noises, a sudden increase of sound like a sharp intake of breath. Or the disk hits another disk. Or there is a vicious *swoosh*, a hard *thwack* and a wild clatter as the opponent's disk is sent flying.

Traffic stops and starts on two sides of their corner. People sit and stand at the curb, waiting for the city bus. Most of them are black people. Most of them are women, and the majority are wearing white uniforms. It is evening. The floodlights are very bright. The Stranahan-Lauderdale Shuffleboard Club is having a tournament. On the back of a large billboard is a notice:

William Pappas in Broward Gen. Hosp. (no visitors) Fred Wike in Holy Cross Room 350 (check hospital for visitors) JIM FLEMING PASSED AWAY— Saturday VIEWING MON. NIGHT 3–5 and 7–9 FAIRCHILDS MASS TUES. SAINT ANTHONY'S 10:30 P.M. "MAY HIS SOUL REST IN PEACE."

The courts are all full. Occasionally there is a subdued laugh. There is the scent of old ladies' toiletries in the air. On a table to one side are the prizes, an assortment of oranges and nuts, marmalades and boxes of cookies. Once a month, during the winter season, there is a "lucky number tournament." One old lady smokes a cigarette held in her left hand as she shoves the cue with her right. Men chew on cigars. Seven old ladies sit to one side in a group. One has a cane. One holds a cue stick in her hand. It has telescoped down into a very short, compact length. She sits there with a wilted yellow hibiscus in her hair, her eyes as expert and as experienced, as cunning as Minnesota Fats'.

A voice:

"I was born in a little town on the west coast of Michigan. A place called Grand Haven. Sometimes I think I should have stayed there."

A mutter:

"You're shootin' the wrong side, Harry."

Some players have delicate cues with lightweight shafts of bamboo. Some have bicycle handlebar grips fastened on the end. Some stoop and aim with careful squints, placing their shots with great finesse, holding their cues with light and sensitive fingers. The scores are chalked on blackboards. The women hang their purses on nails hammered high under the roof shelters, hoisting them up on the ends of their cue sticks.

One set of courts has sidewalls on the edges instead of gutters. This version of the game is called "bumpers." First you hit the wall with your disk and then bounce it into scoring position. You place your bank shots skillfully, either to score or to protect your disk or to block your opponent or to knock his scoring disk out of the way.

Gradually, the games are finished. The players stack their disks into small carriers with handles. People carry their seat pads with them. A man goes around the empty court areas, unscrewing the light bulbs and storing them away. A voice on the p.a. system calls everyone to attention and reminds them of the Christmas party. There is $8.45 in the treasury. Costs are quoted for future social events, for dances and for lucky-number tournaments. Several proposals are put to a vote. A bus pulls up at the corner, its Diesel roaring out its monstrous idle, overwhelming the weak, low-wattage loudspeaker. There are discussions and gestures and wavering cue sticks. Hands are raised. Twenty-seven are in favor of paying $5.50 each to see an ice show. Six vote no. The rest abstain.

In the distance looms a square tower on top of the bank. The time is 8:49. The temperature is 67.

"I'd like to make an announcement for the Sunshine League. We have nine teams signed up. On behalf of the Lucky Number Committee we want to wish you a happy Thanksgiving. Don't eat too much turkey."

They give away the prizes. Names are called. Each winner reaches into a bucket for the ticket of the next winner. People totter forward, make their selections, return and sit down. The pile of wrapped chickens, cookies, and jars of nuts shrinks away. The others sit in their coats and sweaters with their glasses and spit curls and Panama hats. Above the silhouettes of the coconut palms and the cypresses of Stranahan Park the digital time keeps changing.

7 Fly west over Fort Lauderdale. Pass over the beach, the hotels and the money. All those mansions, the maze of residential canals, the inland waterway, and the yachts will sparkle beneath you. Then U.S. 1. Night clubs, automobile dealers, Howard Johnson's. The airport. Small industrial warehouse areas. And then a sea of suburbia, thousands of white roofs lost amidst a bedraggled coconut plantation. The limited-access, divided, multilaned throughway, I-95. More suburbia. Smaller canals. More roofs. More palms. U.S. 441 will flash by, a gaudy, swollen artery clogged with commercial tissue.

After that, the residential areas will begin to thin. There will be broken patches alternating with cow pastures and wooded areas. The Florida Turnpike. Cloverleafs. Overpasses. And then country. Orange groves. Pastures. Wilderness. This is former Everglades country, the sawgrass eliminated, the area crisscrossed with drainage canals, filled with algae and half choked with water hyacinths, a plant originally brought in from Japan as a curiosity. The land is flat, the few aboriginal trees dominated by the melaleucas and the casuarinas imported from Australia to form windbreaks. The Brazilian pepper trees are growing like rampant weeds after having escaped from a doctor's garden. And there are the banyans, the strangler figs, the oranges, from South America and India and Spain.

More pastures. More west. Pioneer City, a frontier town tourist trap that is now defunct. Redneck country. Scene of recruiting drives by the Klan. Dirt roads. Abandoned jalopies dead and rusting. Traffic signs riddled with bullet holes. And then the county incinerator. And then the dump.

Fly in a low circle and you can look down on five acres enclosed within a wall of rocks and dirt excavated from narrow, shallow canals and piled up as a dike overgrown with castor-bean bushes. There is a round pond with a small dot of an island in the center. There is a flagpole in the center of that. There is a small building down there and a row of dilapidated trailers and a swimming pool.

This is the Seminole Health Club. It is a nudist camp. This is where Mabel lives.

Behind the camp's sauna is a red-and-white cabana of striped canvas with aluminum screening and tubular frame, a floor of white sand and a zippered door. This is the Sexy Senile Citizens' Club. There are six members. Mabel is the secretary and treasurer. Axel is the president. Charlie hoses down the place and picks up the trash. Charlie is the oldest. He is eighty-eight, a retired sea captain from Maine who drives down himself every winter.

The major activity of the Senile Citizens is poker. They have a refrigerator, but it isn't hooked up. The hanging lamp fixture dangles by its own wiring from the pipe frame of the cabana. There is an old folding table, lawn chairs of plastic and aluminum. And they play cards. While the younger Seminoles indulge in their passion for volleyball, stretch out in the sun, swim, get a rubdown, overhaul their car engines, flirt, gossip, play billiards and ping-pong, the old-timers prefer the shade. They watch TV in their trailers. They read. They play shuffleboard. They mingle with the weekend crowds, their ruined bodies unnoticed, ignored and yet accepted.

Mabel is sixty-four, fat, wrinkled, and profane. The only thing phony is her teeth. Her husband Axel is sixty-eight, and they have been retired for two years. Mabel was born in Nebraska but worked as a practical nurse in Chicago, where she met Axel, an interior house painter, who was born in Denmark. She is very happy with retirement. She says it is a-okay. But she is too old to have fun anymore. There's no more nookie. Axel has run out of gas. She's had "several offers" at the camp, but Axel "doesn't believe in sharing the wealth." But it's just as well this way. Axel has high blood pressure. "The top of his head might blow off."

Mabel and Axel have been married five years. Together, they get $180 a month in Social Security payments. They have some savings put away, and Axel does odd painting jobs for the Seminoles and occasionally for others. But he has been paying $50 a month alimony for the last twenty-three years. Mabel dislikes Axel's first wife intensely and calls her a "hypochondriac leech" who is hated even by her own daughter. Once she even put Axel in jail. Mabel would kill her like a snake.

Mabel and Axel were part-time nudists when they lived in Chicago, driving to Woodlawn, Indiana, sixty-five miles away on weekends and vacations. After retiring, they went to several other Florida camps before settling here.

Mabel feeds the five camp ducks and the swan early in the morning, followed down to the pond by her dog and her cat. She tends her roses and her hibiscus bushes and the numerous flower beds she has planted. She gets the camp kids to fetch her buckets of manure from their pony. "Horseshit water is the best thing for roses."

Mabel likes all living things. "If they put me in a dark cellar somewhere and left me, I'd still have some kind of flower. Whatever would grow in the dark."

She often goes fishing in the camp's canals. She stands there with a bamboo pole, her blond-gray hair thick, her ample flesh flabby and tanned, wearing nothing but a pair of glasses.

Mabel smokes incessantly and she swears like a sailor. She laughs very often and with a deep sense of irony, especially when she talks about the horde of camp members' children who descend on the place on weekends, referring to them wryly as "the darling little angels." Mabel has two children of her own, six grandchildren and two great grandchildren by her daughter.

Mabel threw her first husband "in the garbage can" when she had "one child in my arms and one in my belly." Much later, when she was fifty-two, she married a nice-looking man of sixty who dressed up like "a banker from Podunk." But two weeks after their wedding he threw his first tantrum, rolling around on the floor, Homburg hat and all, crying like a baby. She said to herself, "Mabel. You done it again." It took her two years to get rid of him. She paid for the divorce herself.

Before her retirement, life was a long series of hassles. She "didn't like life too much" and never knew where her next dollar was coming from. She was nervous and tense and too conscientious, a perfectionist complete with ulcers. Now she doesn't give a damn. She does what she pleases and everything is fine. In her trailer is a little sign: WORK FASCINATES ME. I COULD SIT AND WATCH IT FOR HOURS.

She loves her new life except "there are a lot of crazy drivers in Florida." And the mosquitoes can get very bad. Last summer she and Axel made a trip to Chicago just to get away from them.

She tilts her head back and makes another of her long, loud laughs.

"But still. The only real problem is, no more nookie."

8 His name was Andy Anderson, and he lived in a small frame house on a back street. It was dark green, the interior flamingo pink. The roof was covered with tarpaper. His eyes were bright blue. He was very thin, his mustache white, his voice hesitant and weak. He needed a prostate operation, but he was still thinking it over. During World War I he was classified 4F because he was so underweight. Because of his heavy smoking habit and his frequent colds, he also suffered from emphysema. He was seventy-four.

His first wife died just before he retired. He had five daughters of his own. His second wife had three children from another marriage. For the past eleven years he had been spending his time watching television, reading the paper, tinkering around the house, and sitting on the back porch looking out over his half-acre grove of poinciana trees, which he had planted himself as seedlings. Around 1914 he went to a school in Valparaiso, Indiana, to study telegraphy. But he didn't finish the course. Instead, he got a job as a clerk for International Nickel at Huntington, West Virginia. He then worked elsewhere as a timekeeper. He worked at a shipyard during World War II but then took advantage of the wartime labor shortage to circumvent the age rules, going to work for the Florida East Coast Railroad. After all those years he became a telegrapher at the Fort Lauderdale station. He was also the ticket seller and baggage handler.

Sitting on the screened-in back porch, Mr. Anderson was quiet. There didn't seem to be much to say. He felt he had a lot to be thankful for. Life hadn't been easy. If he had been born with a stronger constitution, it might have been different. He wouldn't have had to take so much guff from the public. And take such a work load. But he had had to stick it out. Jobs were always tight.

It grew quiet again. Andy Anderson stared out at the poinciana trees. And, yes. It had really been worth all those long years of hard work.

"Even if I were in the poor folks' home, I could just sit there and think back on all those memories. You know. And I could say that, well. I tried."

9 The bulldozer trail comes to a sudden end in the middle of a small cypress swamp. Surveyor stakes with bits of colored ribbon are scattered among the uprooted trees, the scarred rocks, the mud and trampled vegetation. You are five miles west of U.S. 441. Ten years ago this was the edge of civilization, but now, even way out here, you can hear the roar of Diesels, the clang of bulldozer pans, the persistent growl of draglines digging still another drainage canal.

Most of this land is owned by the Behring Corporation. Their factory nearby produces standardized, preformed, modular housing units that you can see lined up in a huge storage yard behind a chain-link fence—L's and T's and connecting pieces, all scrawled with painted serial numbers, the windows and doors already in place, the kitchens temporarily cut away from the dining areas, the bedrooms not yet united with the bathrooms, sheets of heavy plastic sealing up the raw ends.

The city of Tamarac has a very narrow, elongated shape on the map, like that of a high-speed, low-trajectory blob splattered from east to west. Tamarac was invented by the Behring Corporation. It grew steadily by a process of acquisition, digestion, and subdivision—section after section, development after development, a forty-acre tract here, a sixty-acre tract there, the angles and squares and rectangles filling in, the whole mass creeping across the landscape like some galactic fungus of concrete and asphalt and white gravel roofs. From out of a modest housing project in the northern environs of Fort Lauderdale it moved over U.S. 441, over the Florida Turnpike and on out into the swamps—sold, promoted, designed, financed, sodded, painted, surveyed, plotted, mortgaged, recorded and deeded, with nothing to stop it until it eventually meets the dikes of the U.S. Army Engineers, the borders of the water conservation areas out in the Everglades.

It is all new. The latest techniques in construction have been utilized. Designers, architects, and engineers have been consulted. It is twentieth-century living, fun-in-the-sun. The bare legal minimum of ten feet is left between the houses. They are lined up in uniform ranks, the colors the same, the roofs the same, cement tile, striped aluminum awnings and fake shutters. Cadillacs are docked inside the carports. Commercial properties line the main avenues, where it is strip zoning, parking-lot deserts, traffic jams, and horrendous signs all over again.

Model homes stand all in a row, colored flags fluttering, name signs in place, a few standard bushes and palms sticking out of the overnight sod: the Mayfair, the

Granville, the Lancaster, the Kenworthy, the Haw-
thorne, the Gladstone. The caravans still roll—a truck
carrying half a roof, a mixer full of concrete, a semi-
trailer load of lumber. Furniture vans pass by. U-Haul-
Its come and go. A truckload of carpets passes a truckload of underground cable. Men with hammers and nail
aprons are up on ladders. Men on aluminum stilts and
wearing khaki shorts are plastering ceilings. Men with
caulking guns are filling in the loose joints.

Golf courses are everywhere. Outside the clubhouses
are the Imperials and Continentals, the tags from Ohio,
Illinois, Michigan, New York, Pennsylvania, and New
Jersey. Inside, all is air conditioning, Muzak, and pecan
paneling. Early in the morning the bar is already in full
operation. Through the picture window you can see the
green. The obligatory golf carts are lined up in a traffic
jam to zoom off at high speeds to the next hole. Because
you can't walk anymore. It isn't allowed. It is too slow
and holds up the game.

A guy strolls inside, swinging a club. You can tell he
is sophisticated by the way he swings it back and forth,
the truly cool way he pokes the door open with the butt
of the handle, one hand still in his pocket.

White golf shoes. Shorts. Flowered slacks. Turt-
lenecks. Short sleeves. Inside the john the silver backing
of the mirror is already flaking off. The edge of the tiled
area behind the urinal is very rough. The plaster is very
thin. The carpet inside has numerous cigarette burns by
the telephone. With one finger you can push against the
wood paneling and feel it buckle. The corpse of a small,
mummified tree frog lies on the aluminum molding of
the glass door. Next to it is a filter-tip cigarette butt.

Go to the section designated Fairhaven 11. See the concrete Jesus on the lawn amidst a flock of concrete birds. See the adult tricycle. This one is equipped with a shopping basket over the back axle. It has two rearview mirrors on the handlebars. A large pink parasol on an aluminum pole shades the rider's seat. And see the canals that meander from bridge to bridge, from pollution to pollution, draining the life out of the Everglades to create dry land on which to build. See the family of blacks sitting on the edge of undeveloped territory, their bamboo poles angling over the bulkhead of concrete slabs. See the toy windmill, the concrete rooster, the plaques of wrought iron, the plastic fish and birds, the mural of pink vines painted on the garage door. Oh, look. The cute nameplates. "Fifty Eight Sixty One" all spelled out so anyone can read it. There are lots of flags on poles. Tiny flower beds are neatly enclosed with concrete curbings painted white. Figurines of donkeys, dwarfs, and flamingos. Christmas-tree balls stuck on the spiked ends of a yucca plant.

The front wall of the Greenhaven 12 social club is a pseudo-colonnade, its fake arches sculpted into the surface. There is a sign on the lawn: BINGO EVERY WED. NITE. On the bulletin board there is a large cartoon that mocks two hippies who sponge on the welfare state, getting food stamps, going to the VD clinic, getting unemployment checks and then demonstrating against the "stinking establishment." A sign advertises free haircuts for shut-ins. There is a phone number. There is a list: 11 WAYS TO KILL A CLUB. You do this by never attending meetings, never accepting posts, complaining constantly but never volunteering for work.

Mainlands No. 9. Notices, rules, and slogans. Folding chairs are stacked. There is a stage, a piano, a flag. There are floor fans and a trophy case, a bingo panel of glass with illuminated numbers. There are reproductions of bucolic paintings, colored lanterns hanging from the ceiling, nine insect-repellent cards, a bookcase and a bulletin board. There is a kitchen behind the Formica counter. A thirty-four-pound dolphin is mounted over a cabinet.

The machines keep moving, the cranes lowering the modules into place. The boxes proliferate into clusters of green, tan, and brown. Canals and ponds are created out of muddy holes. The crushed limestone gets covered with two inches of topsoil and a layer of sod. Crawlers. Draglines. Piles of culverts. Stacks of sewer pipes. Red fire plugs appear among the heaps of dirt and fill. Raw arteries of electric wires and telephone connections stick out of the ground.

At night, far away in the silence, you can hear the faint, intermittent hum of the traffic on the turnpike. And you can hear the steady roar of the drainage pumps as they suck away at the Everglades, spitting the water into another culvert and another canal that leads to one more spillgate, a valve, a discharge, a tidal siphon down to the sea.

The Woodlands is the elite section of Tamarac. The houses start at about $50,000, but many of them are custom-designed and cost much more. There are eight sections in the Woodlands. Five are reserved for adults only, which means no permanent residents under sixteen. All the streets are curved, meandering, complex, leading to sudden dead ends. There is a sameness about the architecture, the colors and the landscaping, but it is tasteful and well done. There are no television antennas, no power lines. These are all underground. There are no fences or hedges delineating property boundaries. The lawns are universally maintained. Someday, when the newly planted trees grow up, it will be a very handsome neighborhood.

All of it is built around the rolling lawns, the ponds, and the free-form design of a golf course. In the middle is a very large artificial hill. On top of this is a tremendous private country club. All is harmonious. All is muted. All is reserved to members only. One day a fifty-five-year-old man was sitting in his electric golf cart with a friend. They were playing the tenth hole when another golf cart quietly drove up. A man jumped out, shot his victim five times with a .38 pistol, jumped back into the golf cart, and returned to the clubhouse. He was on the telephone talking to his lawyer when the police arrived and arrested him for murder.

Beside the social-club pool a woman is stretched out in the sun in a bathing suit. Inside the sliding glass doors an art class is in progress, about twenty gray, white, and blue-haired ladies in artist's smocks sitting in front of their easels.

Rose Wilderman is sixty. She is from Philadelphia, where her husband was a building contractor. They had been coming to Florida for their vacations for about ten years. Seven years ago they retired and moved down permanently. "But a woman never retires. Only a man retires. She still has to do her housework." They came to the Woodlands where Mr. Wilderman acquired a new interest in politics, eventually becoming the mayor of Tamarac. A year ago he passed away.

Mrs. Wilderman finds the Woodlands people very friendly and cooperative, unlike people back north, where everyone simply ignores one another. Here, no one has any real roots, no allegiances except to their adopted community and to their new friends. Despite her original misgivings about living with "old" people, she finds living with her own age group very comforting. Sometimes she misses the young, but she generally approves of the modern atomized family that lives in separate households. It is a mixed blessing, but on the whole the new way is the best. She does miss the opportunity to visit with her grandchildren. She doesn't really miss her own children, however.

Bill Kuipers is sixty-five, a retired sales manager for the Sun Oil Company. A widower, he has no children and never makes return visits north. An exceptionally cheerful man, a serious mood returns only when he talks about the problems facing the nation. He is very much worried, particularly about the current lack of morality in politics, government, and big business. He puts the blame on "big money."

Mrs. Wilderman changes the subject, saying, "You're in Florida now. Forget it. You shouldn't be concerned with the rest of the country."

They both agree that the capacity to enjoy retirement must come from within. You must always be active and involved, and it is important to travel and make visits.

They are both happy in the Woodlands. The weather is good. Transportation is good. But utilities and food are quite high. Medical care is a serious problem. It is very expensive, and for someone just relocating it is difficult even to find a doctor, many of them charging as much as $40 for a couple to come in and be registered as regular patients.

About half of the Woodlands residents are winter visitors only. Of the remainder, roughly 80 percent are retired. The average age is about sixty. The social clubs are very popular. They have parties. They play golf and bridge. They enjoy the art classes, the cooking and discussion groups. They also experimented with educational groups, but it didn't work out.

Coffee and fresh strudel is being served. Pigment and oil is being daubed and smeared, the smell of turpentine strong, the pleasant babble of soft, cheerful voices rising and falling. Someone mentions the superstition some people feel about telling their age. Especially among foreign extractions, it is held to be dangerous to tell how old you are. People will get envious of your health and may try to give you the evil eye. A woman heard Mrs. Wilderman's earlier remark about missing her grandchildren. But she never misses hers. With a broad smile she adds, "Not me. I go to visit them whenever I'm around. But only at my convenience."

An exuberant voice rises out of the gentle murmurs among the mass of easels and stretched canvases, the blurred, half-formed images of waterfalls and forest glens, still lifes, fruit bowls, floral arrangements, sunsets, and marine landscapes.

"Well. This is the way *I* always do golds."

* * *

Advertisement:

SENIOR CITIZENS, INVALIDS—New Portable (hi-rise) Toilet Seat —You now have the opportunity to rent a brand-new portable (hi-rise) toilet seat. Adds four inches to the height of your present toilet seat. Complete safety while in use—will not slip. (Hi-risers) elevate the body so it is easy to arise after elimination.

(bottoms up is our motto)

* * *

He was sixty-one. After eighteen months of litigation with his neighbors, a nine-man crew was sent by court order to clean up the refuse he had been collecting in his yard for years. He opened fire with a shotgun, wounding two of the men, killing another, and killing a bystander across the street. He was declared insane and committed to an institution. A year and a half later, while lying in bed, he opened a vein in his leg with a contraband razor blade. He was found dead.

She was eighty-one. After the policewoman caught her shoplifting, it was discovered that she had been arrested more than sixty times since 1928.

10 She was frowning as she held the
sheet of paper with the lists and the
notes. She sat with her knees crossed, one foot constantly
jerking as she fidgeted with a pen, occasionally patting
her silver-blond wig. But her voice was clear and firm.
She was ready for her report.

Mrs. Hill is a joiner. She is the head of Pocahontas,
Tampa Council #4, a past member of the Order of the
Eastern Star, member of a Golden Age Club, past president of a Grandmothers Club, and a past president of an
American War Mothers Club. She is also a Maharani of
the Shrine Guild, describing her official hat with great
pride. It is a white felt fez with a lavender tassel and
yellow lettering. "It's just gorgeous. All covered with
jewels." The hat cost her $50.

She was very firm about the advantages of being a
member of all these clubs. "I get companionship. Love.
And happiness." Without her organizations, her life

would be "desolate." She has made hundreds of friends through her affiliations and her churches. "I just don't feel right if I can't go to church. I'm not a fanatic. I respect the other fellow's religion. But I do believe in my God and my religion."

When Mr. and Mrs. Hill moved to Tampa on a Thursday, they attended services at their newly joined church that very Sunday. "That's all bunk about retiring and going into your shell and crying your eyes out because you're lonesome. We didn't do that. We went to church right away. I'm a good Christian and I'm proud of it. Happiness depends on believing in God and mingling with Christian people. Nobody comes to see you if you don't go out and make an effort. I could have lived in my house and been a recluse. And been very unhappy. But I didn't." Even today Mrs. Hill sings in the choir. She met her husband that way.

She was married in 1916. She was twenty-one, her husband twenty-three. During World War I he worked as an electrician at the Fall River, Massachusetts, shipyard. He had a high draft number, but he tried to enlist anyway. He was refused. Mrs. Hill was pregnant, and his work was essential to the war effort. Their first child died. They had two more. Mr. Hill became a teacher. He played the violin, the French horn, and the sousaphone. He was a 32nd-degree Shriner and played in the band. On January 22, 1943, his wife's birthday, he suffered a coronary thrombosis. His doctor didn't expect him to live more than two weeks. Mr. Hill was fifty. But he didn't die until he was seventy-seven.

He couldn't move at all the first seven weeks and spent the next two years in bed. Mrs. Hill took care of him at night and hired a nurse during the day. As soon as he was able to travel, they moved to Florida. For five years they lived in Crescent City, a small town near the Ocala National Forest. But it was too cold there. They very nearly moved to Miami, but it was too expensive. Mr. Hill bought a book that showed the number of sunny days per year in different parts of Florida. The Tampa Bay area led all the rest. (The weather is cooler than on the Gold Coast and much dryer. And the *St. Petersburg Times* still gives away a free edition on any day that the sun doesn't shine.)

Life had always been "glorious." She had no regrets and wouldn't do anything any differently. She had lived with one man for fifty-four years and found happiness to be something within. "That sums it up. You make your life around your husband and your children." There were sicknesses and troubles she obviously didn't enjoy. "But I always had a terrific will power. You know. Laugh and the world laughs with you."

She went on at length about the accomplishments of her daughter's children. The boy graduated from Cornell and married a Cornell graduate. He went on to MIT. He saw the work his Uncle Charles had done with vacuum furnaces and decided to follow his work as a materials scientist. He is currently in graduate school.

Very carefully she made sly allusions to her son's work. The space program had just let out a big contract for fifty new tracking stations which will all need new computers. With a broad smile she said, "Charlie's in on the ground floor, boy. But maybe I shouldn't say that."

When she was eight her older sister gave the high school valedictory, and she predicted that someday horseless carriages would be operating all over the world at speeds of ten, twenty, maybe even thirty-five miles per hour. Everyone in the audience laughed at her. The year was 1902.

"But I'd like to tell you about my daughter's oldest daughter. She's twenty-one now. She graduated from high school with honors and now she's at the University of Connecticut. That's where my daughter, her mother, got her master's degree. Charlie also went there for two years. She also plays in the band. All the children play in bands. Now the middle girl got an award for having all A's . . .

"I don't approve of these modern mothers raising all these hippies. Spare the rod and you spoil the child. And yet. Things can always be talked out."

A summary? About her life? If it were to be all chiseled in marble, what words did she have for the world?

Mrs. Hill thought for just a moment, glanced at her notes and said:

"Well. I would just like to say that my baby grand-daughter is making a real name for herself too. She's graduating from high school and she's won three beauty contests. She's on the honor roll. She plays music. She's an expert swimmer. And she's going to go to college. Next year my daughter will have three children in college. I think it's all very wonderful. And I am very proud. And I'm also proud of Charlie and his family and of all the things he's done."

11 Dania takes its name from the Danish farmers who settled there in 1896. It is a town where everyone knows everyone else. It is quiet. It is friendly and small. And yet the crime rate is very high. Dania has had numerous disturbances among the 35 percent of its population that is black. It has had thirteen city managers in seventeen years and eight police chiefs in ten years. When the season is in full swing, the Jai Alai Palace draws 15,000 aficionados every night. And every day 64,000 automobiles go down U.S. 1, which is the main drag.

But it is definitely small. The population is about 9,-800. Fifty-two percent of the city's land is undeveloped. Bypassed by the turnpike, it is squeezed between the Fort Lauderdale airport and the city of Hollywood, cut off from the sea by low land that also belongs to Hollywood and cut off from the west by poor, unincorporated black areas that would make expansion and annexation unprofitable.

But it is famous as the antique center of the South. There are over forty of them—antique shops, gift shops, boutiques, and even a "jeweltique."

In the southwest section, the oldest part of town, many small frame houses can still be seen, some of them with wooden shutters instead of glass windows. One plain white masonry building sits alone in a corner, surrounded by vacant lots. At the rear is a Fort Lauderdale police van. There is a blue and gray Cadillac hearse and another Cadillac hearse in gold and brown. An old black man knocks on the double green door. It opens, and he rolls a gurney inside carrying a long, lumpish object covered with a dark-blue blanket.

Inside the police van is a yellow box marked "E.O.D. for explosives only." There is a small safe with the door ajar and the hinges disconnected, a coil of nylon rope, a pair of rubber boots, a long steel bar which is bent, two full paper bags with yellow forms attached by staples and a stack of small signs: POLICE LINES DO NOT CROSS.

Next to the green doors is a metal trash hopper. Inside there are plastic garbage bags filled with bandages and gauze pads. There is a white linen cover stained by pink liquids and with splotches of dried blood. The door opens. The black man pushes out the rolling stretcher still bearing its cargo. He opens the back of the gold hearse and pushes the stretcher inside, the legs folding up with automatic ease. He drives away.

The front entrance to the office of the Chief Medical Examiner is on First Avenue. In one of the rooms a detective and a hearse driver are both grumbling about red tape and the vagaries of Broward General Hospital.

"They wouldn't let me take the fingerprints off a dead

man. Said I had to get permission. I got a bullet-wound case and they're tellin' *me?* After twenty years?"

"Yeah. They tried to stop me from takin' a body out. Said I didn't look like an undertaker. Look like one? Twenty-eight years and I gotta *look* like one?"

Dr. Mann comes out. On the wall are heavy-duty air-conditioning controls. When the door opens and closes there is the silent sensation of air passing through the room, the faint familiar odor of a meat counter at a supermarket.

Dr. Mann is always busy, his desk littered with forms and reports, his manner professional and humorless. He gets 2,500 to 3,000 cases every year. Right now he has eight bodies on hand, about an average day's work.

The statistics indicate there is a high incidence of homicide among blacks and a very low rate of suicide. Dr. Mann says this has nothing to do with race. It is a matter of social and economic factors. If a study were done on the homicide/suicide rates among lower-class whites the results would be the same. He also challenges that old saw about the home being the most dangerous place. Home is the safest place to be, but the statistics are distorted. For instance, old people do not fall and break their hips. Their hips break first because of osteoporosis, a deterioration of the bones. And *then* they fall. But this is traditionally listed as an "accident."

Suicide among the aged is not extraordinary, but the highest rate is among the twenty-five to forty-four-year-olds. Dr. Mann is intrigued by the large number of suicides that he feels are listed as automobile accidents.

His assistant, Dr. Gable, interrupted.

"Should we do that girl?"

"Oh. I don't think so. Did you feel her neck? The rear tire of the motorcycle blew out and they skidded across the road. She was riding on the back and was thrown up against the wheel of a truck."

The accident occurred this morning. The woman was twenty-two. In a few minutes Dr. Gable comes back.

"I think we better do her. The clavicle is broken and shoved down into her chest."

"Really? Well. Then you'd better open her up."

Dr. Mann volunteers very little information and even less personal opinion. He has to be in court at two o'clock. An old sea captain was stabbed by his wife. It happened in their trailer. He died before he got to the emergency room.

Dr. Mann hands you a 35-mm color transparency. Hold it up to the light from the window. You see a dead face and a number. The features are sallow, wrinkled, old, the eyes not quite closed.

The medical report describes Oscar Williams as seventy-two inches tall. He weighed 230 pounds. He was sixty-six years old. He had minimal arteriosclerosis for his age. The brain was not remarkable. He had marked cirrhosis of the liver. He had emphysema. The blood analysis showed 0.25 percent ethyl alcohol. Methyl alcohol was negative. Dr. Mann says he was stoned. By Florida law 0.10 percent is drunk. There are printed outline drawings on the medical form showing front, side, and rear views of a human body. Old scars have been indicated as well as abrasions. His death wound is marked and described as being elliptical, in the upper mid-abdomen, both backward and upward, five degrees from the horizontal.

Oscar Williams joined the Navy when he was thirteen. He retired as a commander. In 1951 he moved to Ft. Lauderdale and became master of the *Florida State*, a specially designed bulk cement carrier belonging to the Everglades Steamship Company. It was the only one of its kind. It shuttled between Freeport, Bahamas, Ponce in Puerto Rico, New York, and Port Everglades. The crew all lived in Florida, their families always waiting on the dock when the ship tied up. Captain Williams would be standing on the wing of the flying bridge in full uniform, smoking his pipe, his goatee and mustache almost white, tall, broad-shouldered, deeply tanned, tattoos on both arms, smiling down at his wife, Stella, and his daughter, Jo-Gaile.

Less than four years later, in December of 1966, he was master of the S.S. *Green Ridge*, bound for Iran. They were in the Red Sea when he got a radiogram from the Fort Lauderdale Chief of Police informing him that his wife had been shot to death ten days before. They had been married twenty-three years. She was fifty-one.

It took him a week to get home. The ship put in at Djibouti, French Somaliland. He traveled overland for 800 miles to Teheran, from there he flew to Rome, to London and finally Miami. He got home at 2:30 A.M. His house was padlocked. His fifteen-year-old daughter was missing.

The next day he got the keys from the police and found Jo-Gaile staying with some neighbors. He tried to see his wife's killer in jail, but he was refused. Captain Williams spent the next twelve days in Broward General Hospital. His friends tried to provide Jo-Gaile with a nice Christmas. He went back to sea.

But he was in the courtroom February 1 when George W. Stanforth avoided a second-degree murder charge by pleading guilty to manslaughter. Stanforth was an unemployed gas-station attendant. He was forty-five. Captain Williams waited in silence as sentencing was deferred. Very quickly, George Stanforth was hustled back to his cell. Everybody left the courtroom. Without moving, Captain Williams sat there in tears.

Nearly three years later he was once again master of the *Florida State*, carrying a load of cement from Puerto Rico to San Francisco for fuel and then on to Amchitka in the Aleutian Islands. The cement was poured into a drill casing ten feet in diameter and 6,425 feet deep. An armed atom bomb was lowered into the hole, which was then filled. Students all over the country were demonstrating against the test. Ecologists were predicting earthquakes, tidal waves, and polluted atmosphere. Captain Williams said there was no danger. But he spent forty-six days on the island, very worried about the July snows and the 100 mph winds. He brought the ship to San Francisco and flew home. The atomic test proceeded without incident.

On October 27, 1972, at 7:00 P.M., Captain Williams was killed with a twelve-inch butcher knife. His second wife, Barbara Ann, was charged with first-degree murder.

Broward County Courthouse. Room 600. A state's attorney, two deputy sheriffs, and Dr. Mann are just leaving. A skinny woman stands at the clerk's window.

"Come with us."

"What about the subpoena? I was in Haiti."

"It's all right."

There is a shuffling in the hallway in front of the elevator. Dr. Mann is oblivious to it all, engrossed in reading a medical trade paper. Two men are talking about going up to Disneyworld for the weekend. The elevator stops. Everyone files out and moves to Room 347. Someone puts on the lights.

"Can we smoke in here?"

"How long have you been in Florida?"

"Just five weeks, but I lived here before."

"I just love the heat."

Three women sit on the bench. Two scruffy longhairs come in and sit in the back corner. One of the women speaks of a dog in her trailer park who is always breaking his leash. A tall man with white hair comes in, slamming down an attaché case and taking out a leather notebook. The state's attorney comes in. The tall man puts on a pair of black-rimmed glasses and studies a series of colored photographs spread out on the prosecutor's table. The court stenographer enters through a door at the rear of the room.

Everyone waits.

The skinny woman goes out to the john. Dr. Mann reads his paper. The women talk. The hippies murmur. The attorneys study their papers. The courtroom walls are tan, the benches of varnished oak, the ceiling of white acoustical tile with six flush plastic light panels. Up front and to one side are six brown imitation leather chairs in a row. The Florida state flag stands in one corner, the American flag in another. There is a water pitcher on the judge's bench and a rack of rubber stamps.

The judge comes in, saying, "Sit down. Sit down," as

everyone begins to rise. He is dressed in a dark-brown suit and tie that perfectly blends with the decor of the courtroom. He is John G. Ferris. It is 2:20. The name of the defendent is established as well as the identity of the deceased. There is some discussion about which witnesses are necessary. One deputy sheriff is dismissed.

Mrs. Barbara Ann Williams is called forward. She is fifty-two but looks older, her hair in long, iron-gray braids. She wears a blue sweater, an imitation-pearl necklace, and dark glasses. Her white skirt is long and hangs at a crooked angle. It is rumpled and loose. She is a tall woman and wears flat open sandals.

The medical examiner is sworn in. He testifies that he performed an autopsy on Oscar Williams on October 28. The knife blade went into the body five inches. The wound measured seven-eighths of an inch by one-fourth of an inch. Both the colon and the pancreas were cut. The vena cava was severed. There was massive hemorrhaging. He is asked about the height and weight of the deceased. He is asked about the alcohol content of his blood. He says the deceased was drinking "considerably."

The defense lawyer asks for more details about the wound and especially about the degree of the deceased's intoxication. Because of differences in alcohol tolerance, Dr. Mann cannot say for certain if he was drunk. But most people would have been.

Dr. Mann is excused. The next witness is Mrs. Cathleen Denver. It is the skinny woman. She wears wine-colored slacks. Her nose is crooked. Her lips are thin. She is the manager of the trailer park, saw Mr. Williams carried out on a stretcher and talked with Mrs. Williams in the car and again at the hospital. Mrs. Williams was crying. She said her husband was drunk and had beaten her many times. Once he broke her ribs. On another occasion she had to take a room at the Holiday Inn in order to avoid him. She told Mrs. Dever that Mr. Williams had been drunk and very abusive at dinner. She had given him still more liquor, hoping he would go to sleep. Then she went into the bedroom, where she kept a kitchen knife for self-protection. She said she couldn't take being beaten again. He followed her and "walked into the knife."

The defense has no questions. The state's attorney tells the judge that another woman has given a statement to the police, but she called in sick and was unable to appear in court. The judge reads a copy of the statement as the defense attorney murmurs to his client. Barbara Ann Williams' fingers are folding and unfolding nervously.

The next witness is John Clement, who lives in the adjacent trailer. After coming home from work he went out to walk his dog. As he passed the Williams trailer he heard quarreling. A man's voice said, "I dare you to go out." But the windows were closed and the air conditioning was on. He couldn't clearly distinguish any other words of the arguing voices.

The defense has no questions. The bailiff swears in Deputy Carl, who spoke to Mrs. Williams in the hospital waiting room, where he advised her of her right to remain silent in accordance with the Miranda decision. He was in full uniform. There were no promises or threats. Mrs. Williams was under an emotional strain but was coherent and wanted to answer questions. She stated that she and her husband had been drinking and arguing and she had been beaten by him. She told Williams that if he came near her she would kill him. She took the knife with her to the bedroom and there erected a makeshift barricade since the door couldn't be locked. But he crashed through. His wife said, "Here. Is this what you want?" She held up the knife. Williams walked into it. He stood there a moment and then fell.

The defense has no questions. The deputy is excused. A woman sitting on the front bench begins to cry. The judge declares a recess of five minutes and the court starts to clear. A few people have already gone out when the judge speaks to the defense counsel.

"The state informs me that this is all they have. If you would like to call your client back in—"

The state's attorney interrupts with a smile.

"Well. I could show you pictures of the knife."

There is a moment of confusion as the defense counsel goes out into the corridor to call everyone back in. Barbara Ann Williams stands in front of the judge's bench.

"Since the state has not been able to establish probable cause of death, you are hereby dismissed from your bond and your arrest."

Judge Ferris stands up and leaves the room through the door in the back wall.

There is no reaction. Everyone hesitates and then begins to leave. The door opens. A deputy sheriff speaks in a loud, brusque manner.

"Did he turn her loose? I figured he would."

The woman and the two hippies and Barbara Ann Williams go outside and wait for the elevator. Everyone squeezes inside. Mrs. Williams is nervous and on the verge of tears. With restrained bitterness, she mutters to her friend.

"They're *neigh*bors."

* * *

He was seventy-nine. Voluntarily, he surrendered his driving license. There was nothing wrong with him. He just thought he was too old to drive. Two months later he was run over and killed while riding a bicycle.

* * *

He was sixty-three. His car careened through the front yard of a country home as a woman, her husband and friend sat on the front porch. When they saw the car coming, they ran. But he turned a full circle in the yard, first hitting the woman and then her husband. Three hours later, the woman died. He was drunk. And he had a drunk-driving record that went back to 1952. He was sentenced to ten years for manslaughter.

* * *

12 Colonel Bruce is seventy-five. He was born and raised in a little fishing village near Aberdeen, Scotland, and still speaks with a slight brogue. When he was sixteen he lied about his age to join the British Army during World War I and served at the Dardanelles, working at general staff headquarters, doing intelligence work with the local spies. It was his first trip away from home except for a visit to London. Afterward, he went to law school. Upon graduation he got an appointment as a junior attorney in Bombay, India. But his father persuaded him to go to a civilized country, to Chicago, where he had a cousin who was a certified public accountant.

He worked for a firm of lawyers, studying at night at Northwestern University for five years and then becoming a CPA. He worked for several automobile manufacturers, including the Hupp Motor Company. In 1942 the Army commissioned him a captain in the Ordnance

Corps. His job was negotiating tank-construction contracts with General Motors. After twenty-six years of service and a Legion of Merit, he retired as a full colonel. He and his wife moved to Tamarac.

Just before his new house was completed, Colonel Bruce was having dinner with his son, an Eastern Airlines pilot who lives in Miami. He got in the car. But then suddenly he couldn't get out. A blood clot left his leg partially paralyzed.

Cheerfully, he stood up, slapped his left leg smartly and said, "This part is quite dead." He wears a brace occasionally to help him walk.

Colonel Bruce loves his life at Tamarac. He is close enough to see his son and grandson, yet far enough away so he can live his own life. The climate is wonderful. He is always busy. He watches the talk shows and the sports programs on his color TV set. He visits and talks on the phone. He has house guests frequently. He belongs to the Elks and the Masons. He reads a lot. He attends the Presbyterian church in Pompano Beach regularly. His wife drives him around and sometimes friends pick him up. He goes out for lunch. At the social club there is bingo and square dancing, which he can at least enjoy watching. He can't swim anymore but enjoys the pool, hanging onto the side and exercising. Last Thursday he went on a two-day bus excursion to Key West with his cousin and his wife from Scotland who were then visiting.

He has no complaints about Tamarac. In retirement communities like this a person has everything he could possibly want. He doesn't miss young company anymore because of his ailments. Colonel Bruce thinks most peo-

ple just get crabby when they get older. They are bored
and have nothing else to do but bitch.

Life has been great. He fulfilled his ambitions, always
had all the money he wanted and feels very grateful to
Uncle Sam. He has been lucky. He traveled a lot. He has
been happily married. He has no regrets except he has
"this crazy thing," slapping his leg again. He has no fear
of the future and will live as long as he can, happy about
it, enjoying it. He feels dizzy in the mornings and has to
take pills, but he feels all right afterward. About the
hereafter: "Oh. I'm not so sure. At times. If I do die it
won't worry me much. I have had no pain with my leg.
It will be an easy death."

The colonel's house is on an artificial lake formed by
the intersection of several drainage canals. All the houses
and all the roofs are white. Two flags were visible on tall
poles. Thick trees were in the distance. The sky was
clear. The sun was bright. A fresh breeze blew over the
water. Mrs. Bruce came out to speak to her husband.
Even with her hearing aid she is quite deaf, her expression showing a profound nervousness and confusion as
the colonel yelled directly into her face.

He still has a brother and many relatives living in
Scotland. He subscribes to the local newspaper, reading the death notices and the marriage announcements in order to keep track of old schoolmates. He
visited Scotland three years ago on the way to a London rally of the Salonika Army Association. There
were 5,000 men left out of an original 500,000. Since
1917 their group had supported a girls' school and a
boys' school in Bulgaria, which they visited during a
junket to Greece and Turkey. They were wonderfully

treated by everyone who recognized the special badges they wore.

Colonel Bruce considers himself a "now" person. He disappointed his own father, sending money but not returning to live with him in his old age. The colonel still has a seventy-year-old cousin who has never married because his mother won't let him. He believes the younger generation is doing a good job in bringing about needed changes. He saw it in London and in Athens, the same hippies, the same concerns with overpopulation and pollution and war and injustice and the same bad things, the tactics of violence and the drugs. Burning down the ROTC buildings doesn't accomplish anything, although he felt the U.S. should have gotten out of Vietnam much sooner than it did. Why should some young kid lose his life over a rice paddy? Originally, he too thought it was going to be easy. But the United States fell into the same ego trap of the British Empire, wanting to be big brother to the whole world.

He thinks the blacks have been pushed around a great deal. He finds it amazing how intolerant people are of one another. He doesn't understand the mentality of the Irish at all. Scotland is a very Protestant country and yet there are plenty of Catholics, including a lot of Italians. There is never any problem. But the blacks, yes. They really have had a bad time. Just recently a Presbyterian minister in Plantation went out of his way to get some black families to join his church. And several white families immediately quit. Colonel Bruce was very surprised and upset.

But Women's Lib is crazy. Even in Scotland, the men hand over their wages and are then doled out allowances.

Some of these Libbers are just old-maid radicals. They probably never had a man. He just can't understand what it is they want that they haven't got already. They've always been given preferential treatment. Besides, the colonel likes to treat a woman like a lady.

We do have a lousy medical situation here. He is familiar with both the American and the British system and finds socialized medicine much better. When he was touring Scotland he had a set of teeth made for $15. When he came home they didn't fit just right so he had his own dentist reline them. It cost $100. A new set would have cost $450. His wife's hearing aid cost $400. In England they are given away free. It is also true, however, that British taxes are much higher.

He is very much against drugs and would never legalize them. He thinks the death penalty should be retained in order to scare people. But he would liberalize sexual matters. Abortion should be at the discretion of the woman. Prostitution should be perfectly legal. He doesn't think there's that much of a generation gap. Morality hasn't changed. Most women back in Scotland were probably pregnant when they got married. What has changed tremendously is the hypocrisy factor. Things are out in the open now. And he approves. People should be permitted to have full personal freedom.

He chuckled and smiled and remembered being a night student in Chicago in 1923. He went to a burlesque show once and it bothered him for weeks. "To think. With my strong and very strict religious background and there I was, going to see these half-naked women. If my mother knew, she'd turn over in her grave. But gradually I got used to it. And then it didn't matter."

* * *

After thirty-two years of marriage, her husband divorced her. This was the only way she could qualify for welfare benefits. The nursing home cost $500 per month. He had already sold all the furniture. He was $2,000 in debt. His two younger children had moved in with a married sister. He felt guilty about the divorce, but his wife didn't know about it. Dying of multiple sclerosis, she couldn't talk and couldn't understand.

* * *

He was eighty-two. She was seventy-six. They were quiet and peaceful, but they had money problems and were in poor health. They often spoke about suicide. He had warned the manager that she should investigate if their paper had not been picked up by that afternoon. The apartment was unlocked. They were found on twin beds lying on a thick layer of bath towels. There was a note. Her hands were clasped. She had been shot once in the head. He had shot himself.

13 Wray Morehouse sprawled back on the queen-size bed, arms loose and outflung, green-eyed, bare-chested, propped up by a seraglio-type bolster. Socks and dingy, unbleached jockey shorts freshly done at the laundromat were at his side, sorted out and stacked. A leather portfolio was unzipped and spilling out its collection of newspaper clippings and promotional material for the Problem Pregnancy Counseling Service, which he had founded in California. Their regular newspaper ads always began: *Pregnant? Need help?* And there was also the collection of letters responding to an ad for his newest organization, Requiem Associates. The ad ran just once in the *Los Angeles Free Press*. The headline read:

DYING? NEED HELP?

Wray's first experience with suicide came when an old friend invited him over and announced after dinner that he had terminal cancer and this was to be his last evening of life. There were the standard reactions, the denials, the questions, the statements of hope. The son became mildly hysterical, sitting on his father's lap, briefly reverting to the mannerisms of a child. Wray's friend was about sixty. He described him as being "very existential, very heavy-Monterey-woodsy-cold-mist-blown-in-by-the-sea," the kind of guy who lived in a redwood cabin and knew art and philosophy.

Wray listened to the man's profound, calm remarks that represented a lifetime of acquired wisdom. He couldn't remember the exact words but insisted they "were very heavy, not the ordinary breakfast-cereal statements but Chateaubriand statements with béarnaise and with flaming jubilee afterwards." The lights were low. A candle burned. Mozart was on the hi-fi. But there was no special ritual. Wray's friend and his older brother even took up a lifelong sibling quarrel.

There was a pause. "I want you to remember *me*." To Wray, the sound of that final word was like the splat of a "yellow raindrop." His friend's body seemed to disappear, leaving only his eyes, suspended, the room dimming into a black mist, lines of force converging into his pupils like a "vortex of visual experience." The man got up from the table, saying he was going into the other room for a moment. They waited. The record stopped but did not reject. The man's brother got up to remove it. There was a silence. Morehouse chewed on a pretzel that had been overcooked and tasted bitter. Outside on the lawn he could hear a sprinkler whispering softly with a regular sound of intermittent wetness.

"I guess that's it," said the brother. "He's done it." He went into the bedroom and returned. "Yes. He's gone."

The man was lying on a sofa, his head slumped. A fifty cc syringe had been fastened to a vertical stand. A rubber tube led to a needle in his arm. The weight of his falling hand had injected the last of the sodium pentathol.

This happened in 1969. Morehouse had already become familiar with ordinary death ten years earlier while working as an ambulance driver. He had learned how messy and nasty death usually is, how the experience is always botched. "People are clumsy and stupid. It's like peeing on your foot instead of in the toilet." He chuckled. "They miss their chance to take advantage of a really heavy moment."

Wray Morehouse is thirty-one. He is six feet tall and weighs about 155, his hair a little long, his beard short.

He drives a pickup truck filled with tools and pieces of boat equipment and works as a counselor at a private employment agency. He does not smoke or drink. A meal can be peanut-butter on whole wheat or a candy bar or a thermos full of orange juice or an ice-cream soda with four scoops of French vanilla ice cream and heavy chocolate syrup. Every spare minute he has he works on his boat, out there in the Florida summer sun, fully dressed with a black wool watch cap on his head. He said he is working with the desperation of a prisoner digging a tunnel under the walls, fearfully hoping to finish before the guards can catch him.

And yet later he said he "might very well decide to just dock the boat somewhere and go into this whole ethical suicide and euthanasia thing deeply—and go through the TV and newspaper syndrome and the underground acti-

vist syndrome." Ethical suicide parlors, he believes, will
be in full acceptance by 1980, the problems of law and
religious resistance fully overcome. Funeral homes will
have special rooms. Your relatives and friends will say
goodbye to you while you are still living instead of while
you are lying in a state of chemicals and cosmetics. Dying should be made into "a very trippy thing, as trippy
as it can get. I would like to be able to tear holes in time
and space and have people jump through the holes."

Requiem Associates began loosely, gradually, inspiration building on coincidence, experience leading to
form. At first it was something that occurred two or
three times in a year, a word-of-mouth system for doing
the final favor for a friend. But it quickly became a
skilled professional service—the very ultimate in services in an arch-consumer society. The fee varies between $2,000 and $5,000, depending on the specific needs
of the client, the location and the style. Morehouse has
organized an underground group of around a hundred
people. But the inner core consists of only five, each with
his own connections unknown to the other four. They
communicate with one another through a system of
codes and mail drops and public telephone numbers. An
operative may handle a client's request himself or call for
an assistant who will have no knowledge whatever, act-
ing with simple discipline to carry out the assignment.

Wray Morehouse stretched and shifted his position
against the bolster. On the wall over his head was a huge
map of the world. On the other wall was a scale drawing
of the 73-foot boat he was building, having already spent
the previous year working on it, alone. Next to it was a

poster he had found in a head shop. The scene was a tropical atoll at twilight. The sea was placid, a large ketch at anchor. All was in silhouette, all in tranquility. In the corner was the single word "Escape."

He talked most of the night, rapidly, loosely, eloquently, about his boat, about metaphysics, his childhood, his six-year study of psychology at Berkeley and then back to his boat again, the *Golden Rule*, its hull of non-corrosive ferro cement and again, once again, always, back to his theories of death, to the practical and spiritual uses of a graceful, ceremonious, self-willed death, to the aesthetics of it, the silliness, the horror and the beauty.

He hoped that one day something could be done about those insurance clauses that rendered all death payments null and void in case of suicide. If a person had already been medically judged terminally ill, why shouldn't his life insurance still be valid even if he did take the final action himself? No one knew how many people have suffered needless agony in order to be able to leave some insurance money to their survivors.

There were other legal difficulties. Many of Requiem's clients want their bodies disposed of in a quiet, secluded and very private ceremony, without autopsies and without memorials. But there was the problem of death certificates, insurance, Social Security and other death benefits, the probate of a will. These people were advised to cash in their insurance policies in advance; they could usually afford to forego the death benefits. Property was liquidated, common holdings signed over, assets transferred or given away, which avoided the entanglements of probate and also dodged the inheritance taxes.

There still remains the embarrassment of a sudden

disappearance, but so far there had been no investigations. It was easy to make excuses. The person was old and ill. He could have died during a trip or while at a clinic. Moving was also very effective for cutting off gossip. That wouldn't be so unusual. And no one would ever disclose so appalling a family secret. The sheer unreality of it was overwhelming, the suddenness, the finality, the heaviness—all of it emotionally intimidating.

Wray told about the rich man who was stretched out on a bed raised up on a dais, dressed in a hand-made jump suit with hand-sewn shoes of deerskin. Ten people were in the room, including a lawyer, as the man read his own will aloud. The talk and the tears, the farewells and the instructions lasted nearly five hours. Morehouse chuckled again. "It just went on and on and *on* . . ."

But then everyone was asked to leave the room. Five minutes later they were asked to return. The stand and the syringe had been rigged up, the needle inserted, his hand taped to the plunger. The rich man was calm. His wife, silent and still, held his left hand. Other women sobbed. Men stood with watering eyes and tight throats. The rich man said, "This is the moment I have chosen to leave my wife and all of you behind."

He looked at his wife and pushed the plunger, the love and the life going out of his open eyes even as he watched it happening.

And then Wray Morehouse went right into another episode—no hesitation, no chuckles, the one experience that he found too bizarre, still unnerved by it, confused.

"Okay? Ready? Corvette. Salt-and-pepper gray hair. Balding. Thin. Sharp. Woody Woodpecker-type face. Thin mustache. Crow's feet at the corner of his eyes.

Ascot. Coat. Pants. All in very, very poor taste." He was the kind of man who would let the ashtrays in his car get unbelievably full. He was between fifty-five and sixty-five. He was severe, a "very cutting fellow," intolerant, sharp, busy, "with hairs on his ear lobes."

Wray was contacted and asked to call a certain number. A time was set for a meeting at the man's home. Wray had expected a long conference, a discussion of arrangements, advice about legal matters, the question of autopsies, insurance, death certificates. But the man was very quick. He put five thousand dollars in cash on the table and said, "I want your services." Wray was sent out immediately to find the proper place on the nearest freeway, "where I can stack my car up and do it good. I only want to see this place once."

After two hours Wray found the perfect site, a bridge abutment at the bottom of a downhill entry ramp. There was a wide, flat expanse of concrete with a good, clear approach. He wrote out the instructions in exact detail, every turn, every street name. Back at the house, the man looked at what he had written. Wray was told to wait for his wife and then for one other person. And then he was out the door and into his blue Corvette, backing out of the driveway and zooming away.

After an hour the man's wife arrived. Wray introduced himself as a friend and said her husband had stepped out for a few minutes. He didn't know what else to tell her. Nervously he waited, glancing at the telephone. The site was only four miles away, and the police should have already made an identification. Not until later, when he saw a news picture of the wreck, did he learn the car had burned.

And again, that chuckle. "He must have been doing a hundred. I mean, that car just painted itself all over that wall. It was like a mud pie. It was gross. I mean, it was really gross."

The wife's sister arrived, carrying a large leather brief-case. When she told the woman that her husband was dead there was a sharp exclamation that was all at once pain, surprise, and recognition. The sister looked at Wray and said, "Thank you. I think I can handle things from here on."

Another man asked for a location in the wilderness where his body could be cremated in privacy. Wray found a plateau high up in the mountains on the Idaho panhandle that could be reached only by an old logging road. About fifteen people were in the party that formed a convoy of four rented cars. Arriving at the hilltop in the late afternoon, Wray went to work with a surplus trenching tool, scooping out a shallow ditch, filling it with ten pounds of magnesium filings and laying six lengths of pipe across the top. Fifty yards away, the others sat in a circle, on blankets, on folding chairs, one man sitting on an upended suitcase. The air was nippy, and someone built a small campfire. Two hours later everyone got in the cars and drove away, the man still sitting on the suitcase, alone.

He was about fifty-five, robust and distinguished-looking. After a few minutes he stood up and slowly stretched, limping with a severe awkwardness to the edge of the mesa to watch the cars working their way down the mountain. It was twilight. The headlights were on. He watched for a long time, then turned away. He limped over to his suitcase and knelt down, opening the lid and rummaging through the contents, picking up one object after another to fondle it, to study it, to put it down for another. Suddenly he raised a pistol to his temple and fired.

It was a .357 Magnum revolver. The exit wound was enormous, a chunk of bone and hair blasted away, bits of brain splattered on the ground, the left eye dangling. In the suitcase were some clothes. There was an old, well-used hunting knife, a Boy Scout badge, a cracked and dried-out leather belt with two holes torn together. There was an old-fashioned Hamilton double-case pocket watch that was ticking and a framed photograph of a man and a woman standing in time-faded, browned formality.

As Wray described the scene, his eyes became wet, glistening in the light, his voice soft and choking.

They doused gasoline over the magnesium, carried the body over and laid it on the pieces of pipe. They lit the fire, adding gasoline several times before the magnesium was kindled into a low, brilliant flame glowing with a white heat. It reflected on the peaks and the rocks surrounding the mesa and was easily visible to the cars far below, slowly winding their way down to civilization. And then they stopped. It was ten minutes before they started moving again.

Wray and his associate watched the fire for another hour, standing away from the heat and the smell. The pipes melted, the body sinking. Only the charred torso was left when they checked the horizon for strange cars and then camped out for the night under blankets.

"The stars were fabulous. It was a moonless night. I really dig stars and birdies and fishies and things like that. In the morning there was nothing left but white ashes. We stirred them around and only saw bits of metal."

Invariably, when Wray referred to his clients, he talked about "helping them." He said he always stopped on freeways to help people change flat tires. He said he enjoyed the warmth of their gratitude. But Requiem was not just a matter of assisting people through their physical agonies. He saw himself as a bringer of life rather than as an agent of death. And he was convinced that he had a mission. He would not say whether or not it was divinely inspired. He was reluctant to admit that he believed in any kind of hereafter, always slipping away from the question.

Wray admitted having a strong personal fear of dying by accident and dying by violence. And then he said, "The ultimate act of any god is to determine his destiny. To die at a moment of choice is to increase your chances in any kind of destiny that you seek in an after-life—if there is one."

But one does have to prepare for the hereafter. "There is an infinitude of possibility when you die. If you can think infinitely, then you will be able to select. You will not be blinded by the categorical representation of infinity."

He didn't know what state of spirituality he had thus far attained, but his boat would definitely extend his qualifications. Building it with his own hands and sailing it around the globe, lying under the stars, listening to beautiful music and contemplating the universe—all of this would promote a great internal expansion.

The talk went on with only occasional pauses to go to

the john, to take a call from a girlfriend who was in a local psychiatric hospital, another call from her doctor, who wanted to know the extent of his emotional involvement, a trip to the kitchen for peanut-butter sandwiches, through a sea of tools and boat-building materials piled high in the living room. There was a discussion of theories, destinies, star gates through the space-time continuum, the cosmic consciousness of the sun, the infinite varieties of gods in the many universes. He told about his sexual and spiritual liberation at twenty-three, when he had his first "free-and-rolling-down-the-hillside-full-of-flowers experience" with a faculty member's wife at Berkeley. He told about the free-form dancing that he did when alone, exploring his universe, especially the space behind him. Most people didn't know what was behind them and usually danced all out in front. He gave examples, his arms and hands making sinuous motions, first behind his back and then in front of his face, gestures somewhat like those of Balinese dancers. And he demonstrated his personal symbol of consciousness, an infinity sign formed by his cupped hands and crossed wrists.

Morehouse was fascinated by the manifestations of phallicism he saw all around him—the tall commercial buildings erected to the glory of some robber baron's genital fantasy; the ads for liquid detergents that show the tip of a plastic bottle ejaculating into a housewife's hand. He was convinced that Madison Avenue psychologists have deliberately designed the shapes, the concepts, the names, even specifying the exact consistency of the detergents so that they would duplicate the exact consistency of sperm. He frequently mentioned the double-arched "M" of McDonald's hamburger shops, admitting that the two semi-ellipses could resemble a pair of female breasts or even buttocks but insisting the real intention was to symbolize two erect penises.

He was very impressed by the Tibetan *Book of the Dead*, but *The Urantia Book* was his favorite. He read from the fly leaf: "Your world Urantia is one of many similar inhabited planets which comprise the local universe of Nebadon. This universe together with similar creations make up the super universe of Orvonton—one of the seven super-evolutionary universes of time and space which circle the never beginning, never ending creation of divine perfection. . . . death is only the beginning of an endless career of adventure, an everlasting life of anticipation, an eternal voyage of discovery."

As he thumbed excitedly through the pages to find some specific passage, Morehouse said he didn't really believe all of the book, but he modulated its message to go with his own experiences. Later he referred to Jesus being but one of 602,000 bestowed sons known as "Michaels." Looking up in befuddlement, he said he knew there was that precise number because "They say so in the book."

Morehouse described two of his cases who died by inhaling the fumes of prussic acid and were buried far at sea in special bio-degradable black iron containers. One of them was a woman who got seasick on the way out.

Long after Requiem Associates had been established, Morehouse decided to present the philosophy and the ethics of suicide to the public. He bought space in the *Los Angeles Free Press* and published an announcement

that was half ad and half vanity-essay. He claimed to
have received 25,000 queries from the one insertion, reading aloud from a dozen letters. He also read the inquiry
he got from the Better Business Bureau.

But by taking out the ad he also blew the whistle on
himself. He insisted that the Tampa police had him under surveillance, although they had never actually ques-
tioned him. He was certain his phone was tapped. Once
he heard voices and noises on his line. He said they
tapped into his neighbor's phone as part of some fantas-
tic mixup. He said he had the telephone people come out,
and they found that the insulation on his wires had been
cut.

He had to curtail his activities. Because he was very
security conscious, any inquiries had to be referred to his
associates by a special system of secret communication.
"Some asshole cop" must have tipped off the local reporters. Items suddenly appeared one day in both the *Tampa
Tribune* and the *Tampa Daily Times.*

Most of his cases were routine. One man did look as
though he might not go through with it until Morehouse
asked him very pointedly if anything was wrong. One
had a wild party, only a select few of the guests invited
to stay afterward. Morehouse didn't know of anyone
who requested a special meal. But he had heard of one
man who insisted on making love as he died. It cost a
fortune to hire a willing and beautiful prostitute, but
Requiem Associates did arrange for him to die in the
midst of an orgasm.

He was vague about the number of suicides he had
counseled. Between sixty and eighty, he said finally.

"My feeling is that the decision of the individual and

whether that decision is exercisable or not is the most important issue. A mother should not be a mother unless she wants to be. As far as I'm concerned a child entity is not really that much of a person even for four or five years after it is born."

Wray Morehouse's own sister died at about five. He was a few years older. He had given her the mumps.

On the previous evening he had described his mother as a hypochondriac who had killed herself. A moment later he was speaking of her in the present tense. But then it seemed she was indeed still alive.

He referred to a simile the Rosicrucians had about the lower orders of consciousness in the universe: "A horse is a man running. A bird is a man flying. A fish is a man swimming. Did you ever look at a little birdie and just *become* a birdie? I like birdies."

But then he was reminded of his own story about the ugly bird that kept flying around his boat. He had called it a species of cunnilingus Americanus and threw a bolt at it, breaking its leg. "But that bird was so *ugly!*" he exclaimed, surprised, trying to laugh it off. "But actually. That was just a sporting thing. I'm always throwing things. It was a hunting instinct. I felt terrible when I finally hit the bird. I felt awful."

*　*　*

He was fifty-five. He got drunk, had an argument, and threw his wife and four children out of the house. His son called the police. At the station he was submissive as they did the paperwork. They put him in a holding cell. A half hour later they found him hanging by his belt. He was revived and taken to a hospital. Now he is paralyzed from the neck down.

*　*　*

He was fifty-six. He walked into a grocery store just as two armed robbers went in. The proprietor pulled a pistol and fired four shots. He was hit twice and killed.

*　*　*

14 When he was twelve, he was very good at dancing the Charleston. He was small for his age, about the size of a six-year-old, his mother never able to get stylish clothes that were small enough. His uncle, a maître d' at a big hotel in New York, thought it would be kind of cute if he danced at the Pall Mall Club for the New Year's Eve party.

Arthur Bourbon was scared. He had been raised as a Catholic, so strictly he wasn't even allowed to go to movies. And there he was, in his little sailor suit, ogling these laughing, drunken women in their short skirts, their long beads, their ostrich feathers and furs, the towering, loud men in their tuxedos. Everyone was applauding, but this was the first time he had ever danced on a waxed floor, his feet slipping and sliding so much he had to dance like a madman just to keep up with himself.

That frantic Charleston became his very first audition, dancing so fast he stepped and kicked and smiled his way right out of his childhood. Because a woman at the party, who operated a dancing school, offered him a scholarship for a year. Arthur didn't really want to go. Instead of studying six days a week he wanted to go out and play with the kids. But eventually he got used to it, and then at sixteen he was given a lifetime scholarship. His benefactress got him jobs at clubs and at hotels.

In high school he auditioned again, this time at a drama academy. He had been tutored for the audition by an old actor, but Arthur was dissatisfied. Very impressed by a recent prison movie, he was determined to improvise his own thing with a handkerchief containing a chopped-up onion. Clutching his number in his hand, he shivered his way onstage, still uncertain whether to play it his way or to play it straight. He blew it completely, and yet—two of the winners later dropped out, the judges had been impressed by his audacity and by a certain raw something he had displayed. So he got the scholarship. He quit school and studied dramatics full time—modern and ancient theater, Chinese drama, the construction of stage sets, radio, and costumes. At the end of the first year he got still another scholarship. After that he was given a job teaching pantomime.

He was in show business for thirty-three years, living out of his suitcase, never settling down, never marrying. In New York he sang and danced at Billy Rose's Diamond Horseshoe, in *High Button Shoes* and *South Pacific*, at the Latin Quarter with Sophie Tucker, with Carmen Miranda. Every year at the Clover Club in Miami he was billed as "the world's fastest tap dancer." And he had his own act, Bourbon and Baine, until his partner suddenly quit to become a nun. He had even performed once in front of Al Capone at the old Hotel Deauville on Miami Beach.

Then he retired, coming to Florida fifteen years ago, remaining active with odd jobs, teaching ballroom dancing to senior citizens at the City of Hollywood Recreation Department, singing at churches and once in an opera in Miami with Renata Tebaldi.

Arthur Bourbon was a little pudgy. His face was pink. He wore glasses. But he was very energetic and talkative, and you would never guess he was sixty years old.

Until four years ago he had his own house but was seldom in it because of his activities. Then he moved in with his sister, a widow who had just retired from the telephone company and moved from California to Tamarac. Arthur and Natalie hadn't seen each other in thirty-one years.

And then he started *That Old Gang Review*, gathering together all the local talent—friends of friends, his sister, a pianist who was eighty-one, a chorus girl Arthur had worked with in *Oklahoma!* whom he found quite by accident in a church choir. They put together a variety show and offered it to retirement-community social clubs. They arranged their own music, a piano their only accompaniment. They designed and made their own costumes and made a deal with one Tamarac social club to give them a place to rehearse in exchange for a free show.

They played eighteen clubs and condominums. A building inspector in the troupe tacked up notices everywhere he went and handled the bookings. At first they performed for free. Later, someone gave them $50 from the recreation fund. Then they got $150 a performance. It was for all seventeen of them, but at least it paid for their gas. In every case they got a standing ovation, except once. By then they were so spoiled they were heartbroken.

Arthur Bourbon talked about traffic and pollution. He enjoyed modern things but yearned for the old-fashioned: a big frame house with a fireplace and a wide front porch. He could live quite happily with gas lamps. He regretted the passing of the old ways, horses and buggies, bare feet, baskets of fruit and fresh vegetables.

He made several references to "getting it someday" and being able to "get away from everything" where he would be able to live in a rustic setting in the mountains in a warm climate. He would not say where. Natalie smiled, saying, "We're getting dramatic now." But again he dodged the issue with a quiet "I'm looking into a few things." Natalie said, "I want people." Arthur said, "Not me."

Finally, he told it. In a week he was going to a Trappist monastery in Conyers, Georgia, hoping to be accepted as a monk. If they refused him, he was going to try again at The Hermitage of Our Lady of Solitude, a single trailer parked somewhere in a remote section of Texas. He would love to live alone and in silence—the beginning of his true vocation, his first chance to give back some of those gifts granted him by God.

And he felt that it had all been divinely arranged, all of it, the final explanation of all those freak opportunities that had come to him so easily all his life. As he got older dancing had become harder, so he decided to take some singing lessons. Suddenly he developed a voice rich enough to enable him to sing solos in churches. And it was this that might give him the edge in being accepted by the Trappists. They had a special choir of monks who rose at two in the morning, singing their way into the chapel with candles.

And he did it. He went up to the Monastery of the Holy Spirit. He stayed three days in the guest house, was interviewed by the Vocation Master and was granted an audience with the abbot. But they already had too many old men. They would accept no one over forty-five.

But the rules had been relaxed since the second ecumenical council, and this monastery had always been the most liberal of the Trappist retreats in the United States. Hoods were no longer required. Three meals were eaten instead of one. Silence was maintained only at certain hours and in certain areas. Sometimes movies were shown and sometimes television. They were about to celebrate a jubilee for monks who had been there for twenty-five years. Their families had been invited to come up and visit, the first in half a lifetime. In fact, the abbot was very much concerned at that moment with his entertainment problems.

Something stirred when Arthur Bourbon heard that old word. He pleaded to be permitted to help with the entertainment and also to be allowed to demonstrate his fitness.

And this was how Arthur Bourbon made his final audition, with God himself in the audience. A divinity student gave him his musical accompaniment, playing "Ida, Sweet as Apple Cider" on the organ. It came out like a Bach fugue. And he danced. He danced for his soul. He did the finest soft-shoe shuffle of his career, his highest butterflies and rollovers, his fastest buck-and-wings, his elbows and knees jabbing toward the heavens, his smile beguiling the angels.

Afterward, he almost choked, trying to catch his

breath. He couldn't get offstage to pant and wheeze behind the curtain in private. There was no stage. There was no curtain. And he didn't dare let them see how winded he was. There was an awkward moment. The assembled monks had never seen anything at all like this before.

And then they applauded.

He spent another night in the monastery, this time sleeping in one of the cells. The next day the Trappists accepted him.

Phase One of the Hawaiian Gardens condominium apartments was built in old pasture country. Across the road was a holdout: old sheds and fences and gates, trees and a skinny horse.

There was a long delay. There was no stage, and the floor was covered with a shag rug. The main room was octagonal, with four doors leading to four other rooms, each with a neat sign: CARD ROOM—EXERCISE ROOM—HOBBYSHOP—BILLIARDS. In the center was a dance pit filled with chairs and a twittering, chattering audience, all dressed in bright clothes, stripes and bells and loud colors. The ages ranged from distinguished to decrepit, with a small sprinkling of grandchildren with braces on their teeth.

Members of the troupe and the club were busily hanging up a temporary curtain to cover the door to the Exercise Room. The pianist went over some last-minute changes. The microphones and wires and switches were snarled and unsnarled, tested, adjusted and then readjusted when some went dead and others weewahed with outrageous ultra-register decibels. There were some announcements from the entertainment exchange. Some extraneous recorded music cut in. A man ran offstage, and then the mike went dead. The announcer dropped the mike on the floor. The audience went on with its loud, constant chatter. Finally, details were given about the club dinner and the fishing trip, the boats and the lunches. The chattering resumed. There was another announcement:

"We have an unusual request. Since there is no stage and no dressing rooms, everything has to be improvised. The men and the women in the troupe are using the johns as dressing rooms, but they are being interupted by people constantly coming in to go to the toilets. Please. As a favor. Would everybody hold your water? Thank you."

There were giggles.

"Also, on July Fourth there will be pot-luck night. Ten people will be seated at a table. Setups will be provided. 'F' Building is host and hostess for the month. And whoever is spreading rumors that the entertainment committee goes out of business in July, forget it."

Arthur appeared, dressed in a pearl-gray double-breasted suit with high, wide lapels. He had a pink shirt and a pink handkerchief in his breast pocket. He was introduced as "Arthur Bourbon from the Diamond Horseshoe. I think you'll have a nostalgic evening."

He was smooth and slick. He asked if anyone there was from California. When he saw the hands the piano began playing and he began singing "California, Here I Come." Chicago? "Chicago" is my kind of town. And on to "Beautiful Ohio" and "Dixie." Great cheers from the audience for "The Sidewalks of New York." No one was from Montreal, but he sang "Alouette" anyway, everybody joining in and giggling when he slapped his behind at "c'est la derrière." He did a Maurice Chevalier number, went off and came back to introduce the troupe, which came out of the Exercise Room to dance and sing their way over the shag rug, the men dressed in solid-color shirts with white pants and shoes and white satin vests, the women in pastel dresses with matching shoes and chiffon scarves.

A man did a solo, "Without a Song," his voice uncertain, the piano missing a little as it tried to follow. The mike went dead while he was singing "A Beautiful Lady in Blue." Arthur Bourbon came out in a whirlwind dance, a female dummy in his arms, its feet attached to his shoes. There were laughs. He announced into the mike, "I'm not out of breath. It's out of me." The young ex-chorus girl did a torch song—"Lay Your Head on My Pillow"—and then "Joe." A couple did a Mary Martin number from *South Pacific*. She was dressed in a grossly oversized sailor suit, singing, "I'm five feet two, eyes of blue" as he came out in a grass skirt, a mop wig and coconut shells for bra cups, with twirling tassels attached. Then a woman sang an aria from an operetta.

Bourbon came out again in a straw skimmer and a red and white striped jacket. He recited a poem, did a soft-shoe shuffle and brought on the entire troupe dressed in old-fashioned bathing suits and straw hats and fake mustaches to do "On a Sunday by the Sea." A fat woman did a comedy skit with a small man who wore a Marx Brothers wig. She threw him around in Apache style, carrying him offstage over her shoulder. The fat woman ran back out into the audience to kiss all the men. The audience was hysterical.

Then Bourbon got four volunteers and directed a hat-decorating contest, two men digging feathers and fake flowers and veils out of two boxes to fasten it all on basic hats that two women were wearing. As the piano went into "Buffalo Gal," the women sashayed around in their fancy millinery. Then it was the men's turn, the women dressing them in false eyes, wigs, hats, and scarves. All four paraded and got their applause. Bourbon had them line up on their elbows and knees and repeat after him, "I know in my heart, I know in my mind, that I have got a stuck-up behind." The audience shrieked.

Their singing star did an Italian aria as the pianist tried to do her justice. There was applause and a few "bravos." She did some Victor Herbert, went off and reappeared in a wide hat with plumes to sing another number. As she and Bourbon finished up with a waltz, they kicked the wire, and two men leaped up with alacrity to catch the tottering microphone stand. Vicki and Arthur ended up in a short duet.

Bourbon read a poem called "Getting Old" which compared a person to an old house with a changing roof, dim windows, and a shaking foundation.

> But I am not my house
> Only the dweller
> Don't mix my house with me.

Then Arthur Bourbon announced that this was to be the last performance of *That Old Gang Review*. He gave no explanation. There was no reaction from the audience. And then the whole gang did a long medley of numbers, Bourbon directing them with hyperactive hand movements.

". . . if I can give . . . to live and to give of one's self . . . this is a great country . . . hats off to America . . . land of the free and the brave . . . America, I love you . . . from ocean to ocean . . . a hundred million others like me . . ."

The young woman, the ex-chorus girl, came out in regal dignity, wearing a Folies Bergère patriotic costume as the group sang:

". . . there she is, Miss America . . ."

Bourbon finished it off:

"Thank you for a lovely evening. May God bless you and keep you. On my salary I can't afford it."

There was loud applause. But no standing ovation.

After the show at the Hawaiian Gardens Phase One, he announced to the audience that he would be glad to teach anyone to "do the discotheque." Please go to the center of the floor and make a circle. The chairs had already been cleared. The confused old ladies held hands, thinking probably that this was to be another folk dance. He showed them how to loosen their elbows, their knees and their necks. The ladies were hysterical, their bosoms shaking one way, their rumps another, their feet fast and confused as they giggled and squealed.

Natalie was off in one corner, dancing by herself. She explained that her brother had another week before going back to begin his thirty-day postulancy. If accepted he would then come home to settle his affairs before returning forever, taking his simple vows and eventually his solemn vows.

Natalie said it had been a very tough audience, which was why they had failed to get a standing ovation on this, their final performance. She smiled and looked around, whispering hoarsely, "They're all a bunch of Jews. They wouldn't stand up for Moses."

Arthur Bourbon was in the center of the dance pit, surrounded by the clapping, giggling old ladies and a bamboo fence. It was his very last performance, his last night in show biz, his joints loose, his arms gracefully doing the Swim, the Monkey and the Frug, his legs limber, his feet clever, his body joyous with the beat of the music, his head bobbing back and forth, smiling with the glow of some ultimate serenity.

*　*　*

He was seventy-eight. He had never married. But he met a fifty-three-year-old woman who took care of him for five years, did the shopping, went on errands and helped him to the doctor's office. He gave her money and a car. Then he had a heart attack. When they told her he would die in a few days, she forged his signature, got it witnessed, cleaned out his bank account, emptied the safe-deposit box, and disappeared with $26,000. Five months later she was caught and pleaded guilty. The money was already spent. After four more massive heart attacks and one stroke, intensive care, repeated predictions of immediate death, he hobbled into the courtroom. She was put on probation.

*　*　*

He was eighty-six. He drank boiling-hot coffee and moonshine. He ate gherkins and raw hamburger. He lived in the rotting remains of an abandoned shark boat and wore a ragged beard.

He had been a fisherman and a boat builder, a rumrunner and the captain of a towboat. But he had influential friends— owners of Cadillacs and Imperials who would drive into the mangrove thicket to sit under kerosene lamps and drink and tell stories and eat his famous oyster stew. Everybody knew him. In certain bars he never had to pay for a drink. He could walk over the causeway to the grocery store where he did his shopping on credit. And if he got too drunk he could stay for free at the ancient motel across the road. One night he didn't feel well and stayed over. They checked him in the morning. He was dead.

15 The planes come in, circle, lower their flaps and wheels, cut back on their throttles, bump, throw the jets in reverse, screech and bounce over to the terminal ramps. Taxis. Baggage carts. Conveyor belts. Announcements over the loudspeakers. Winter season. Holiday season. Summer season. The rates go up and down. The passengers embark and disembark. Sandals. Shorts. Business suits. Slacks. Sport shirts. The planes leave the way they arrive. They carry passengers and mail and freight. But every plane that leaves Miami also carries one or two secret passengers on board. They are dead. Encased in their caskets, they are stowed away with the cargo and the baggage.

A leading funeral director reports that 35 percent of his clients are flown back north for burial. It used to be even higher, as much as 45 percent. It costs between $500 and $750 more to ship a body for a funeral up north. The local undertaker provides the casket, gets the death certificate and tends to many other details. He schedules the flight and provides the transportation. Arrangements are made with the undertaker up north who will take final delivery.

The air freight itself costs $23 per hundred pounds. Casket and remains average 400 to 500 pounds, and the total bill runs between $80 and $120. It must be paid in advance. The casket is delivered an hour and a half before departure time, before the living passengers begin to board.

Cremated ashes, however, can be mailed by parcel post. It costs $2.80 in postage. In order to get a receipt, they are usually insured for the minimum $50. This is one of the reasons why more than 30 percent of the funerals in south Florida use cremation, compared to the national average of 4.6 percent.

Cy Case is thirty-six. His original name was Caserio. He is half Irish and half Italian and for business reasons decided to shorten his name to Case. He has been in the undertaking business ever since he was an eighteen-year-old student at Fort Lauderdale High School. Before graduation the seniors were placed as temporary apprentices in various trades as part of a vocational experiment. Just for the hell of it, Case and a buddy picked the funeral business. Both of them are still in it.

Case is considered something of a renegade by the more conservative members of his profession because he believes in public relations and advertising and in modern accounting methods. He knows all about mergers and leases, stock-distribution angles and financial ma-

neuvers. He loves big business, so much so that undertaking itself is really secondary.

Case merged with and then took over the Baird Funeral homes and now uses the name Baird-Case. There
are only three funeral corporations that are publicly
owned in this country. Two are listed on the American
Exchange: International Funeral Service with ninety-
nine homes, fifteen cemeteries, five mausoleums, four
crematories, one ambulance service, and gross annual
sales of $28 million; and Service Corporation Interna-
tional, with 104 funeral homes, thirty-eight cemeteries,
five crematories, and sales of $59 million. Baird-Case sells
over the counter. There are 280,000 shares outstanding.
There are ten branch funeral homes. In 1971 they did an
annual gross of $1,350,899. There are forty-seven em-
ployees and 249 shareholders. The 1971 low bid was 6½.
The high was 9½.

Mr. Case encourages people to visit his display rooms.
He says it is not true that the living always pick out the
cheapest for themselves. He has 2,000 names in his files
of people who have already made "pre-need" arrangements. This represents roughly $2 million worth of busi-
ness. But the state of Florida does not permit undertakers to accept deposits. Still and all. People come in just
the same and record their preferences and their deci-
sions. A seventy-five-year-old woman had come in only
a few days before to choose her own casket. She made her
arrangements with an attorney for the kind of service
she wanted, the kind of priest, flowers, procession, grave
marker, and public notices.

Sit there in his office and listen as Mr. Case explains
it all. He is dressed in a black suit with a black tie, his

hair short, his shirt white. His secretary holds his calls. He is very good at quoting statistics, costs and facts, only occasionally pausing to reach for a book to check himself.

There are 22,000 funeral homes in the United States, and they gross $2 billion in annual sales. By 1980 it is projected that the annual gross will reach $3 billion. Eleven years ago in St. Petersburg there were eleven funeral homes. Now there are twenty-six. The national average cost of a funeral is currently $962. Baird-Case charges an average of $886. Funerals for children are less expensive and almost never render a profit.

The tombstone business is virtually extinct. Nowadays the cemetery lawns must be mowed by big machines because of the labor costs, and only flat tablets of bronze are permitted. Paupers without families are never cremated because Florida law states that there must be a signed authorization. If the pauper is qualified, Social Security will contribute $255 toward his funeral. The Veterans Administration will pay another $250. Baird-Case's minimum fee of $475 includes a box, cremation, an urn, the service, transportation, and embalming. Embalming is always necessary. Florida law prohibits cremation before forty-eight hours after death to allow for autopsies, possible investigations of foul play or other inquiries. The law also says that after twenty-four hours, embalming or refrigeration must take place, and since there is no space available for refrigeration—hospital morgues are very small and it is too expensive for a funeral home—embalming precedes the cremation. It really isn't necessary to have any container for cremation except for the sensibilities of the personnel at the funeral home. In a no-view service a simple pine box is used.

When Jessica Mitford's book *The American Way of Death* appeared the funeral industry was thrown into a furious panic. But Mr. Case remained calm. When he addressed various civil groups he managed to cover the subject quite well in a five-minute speech. His point was that if he were to do business out of a small office in one of the commercial warehouse districts in town, if he used a basic station wagon instead of an $18,000 Cadillac hearse, if he could omit the embalming, if there were no viewing, if funeral services were conducted in the front office with a plain wooden box set up on a couple of sawhorses, then, yes, indeed, he could perform a funeral service for the kind of price Jessica Mitford was talking about. But just how many people there in the audience would want to hire him and his services then to bury one of their relatives? And that of course shut them all up immediately.

There is more:

The national annual death rate is about 9 per 1,000 population. In south Florida it is 11 per 1,000. In 1971 the highest rate in the country was 13 per 1,000, in Tampa. Undertakers are sometimes sued for malpractice if any sort of mutilation occurs. Indigent cases are rare in Broward County, which pays out only about $8,000 per year. This is reimbursed by Social Security. The county pays the funeral director $250 and provides space in a municipal cemetery. A welfare department case worker supervises the proceedings, inspects the simple cloth-over-wood casket, and approves the clothing. There is no service. The graves are unmarked, but records are kept of the locations. If the deceased is a veteran, a special bronze marker is provided by the government. By law, a body cannot be held for payment. It is customary to expect payment within thirty days. But funeral homes catering to black people insist on payment in advance. Mr. Case himself writes off about 1 percent of his business as bad debts. He is now beginning to see a lot of drug-overdose cases. But there is no truth in the idea that cremation is necessary because of the shortage of real estate. You can bury 1,000 people in a single acre of land. That means that the population of the United States could fit into roughly 313 square miles. The population of the world would need 6,250 square miles, a cemetery two miles wide that stretched from Fort Lauderdale to Seattle.

Mr. Case speaks of the modern art of embalming that began in this country during the Civil War when the battlefield dead were commonly shipped long distances for burial. Formaldehyde was used then just as it is now, although glycerine and perfume may be added. The fluid comes in sixteen-ounce bottles in concentrated form. He mixes six ounces per gallon of water and needs two to three gallons to fill the complete arterial system. The process is simple. Blood is pumped out of one vein as the fluid is pumped into another. The needles can be inserted anywhere, into the neck, the arm, even the foot. Every embalmer has his favorite place. In the old days the job used to be done in bathrooms or in farmhouse kitchens, but now a professional laboratory is used.

Then the intestines are drained with a long, large needle connected to a tube and a pump. The cavity is filled with full-strength formaldehyde inserted with the same needle. But you must always be careful not to overembalm. Sometimes the protein in the muscle is dried out too much. The eyes might open and the lips could crack.

But real skill is involved in the restorative arts. The mouth must be closed with a lump of wax behind the lips or even a piece of wire intricately fastened between pins inserted into the jawbones and into the upper gums. Mr. Case has a special tool for this, the same one used by surgeons. But closing the mouth is not enough. A suitable expression must be created. The lips must be artfully composed. And then the cosmetology, the powders and paints, the waxes and putties, the lacquers and rouges, all used with sensitivity and imagination.

Ah, but bullet wounds!

The entrance hole is nothing. A plug of wax, a little powder, and it is easily covered. But the exit wound is the thing, the hole large and gaping with jagged edges and loose fragments. Still and all, it's not so tough if someone commits suicide with an ordinary caliber pistol and holds it to his temple. Wax and cosmetics, a certain amount of artificial hair carefully selected to match the color and texture, the wax stippled with a towel to duplicate the skin pores—even a pistol shot in the mouth isn't too bad. But one guy used a hunting rifle, a 30/30. His face just disintegrated. Everything came loose.

Suddenly, you aren't listening to Mr. Case, the Waspish establishmentarian. The Irish is beginning to come out. The Italian is coming out. It is Cy Caserio's big frame that has leaned forward out of his chair, his arms upraised, his hands quick and demonstrative, his voice excited as he tries to push the ruins of that face back together in mid-air, as he still labors over that mutilated ghost that hovers there over the desk, trying to restore its image, to maintain the illusion of its being alive, to convince himself of that very form and order and sequence of effect which that other man must have ceased to believe in when he put that cold, hard tube into his mouth, his tongue seeking out that small, grooved hole that reached all the way to the eternity that he tickled and triggered with his toes.

There is a pause. The funeral director leans back in his chair. Shotgun? Like Hemingway? Forget it. There's nothing left.

And all of this labor and expense, this artistry, these props, these tools and materials go into providing a ritual scenario called The Viewing. It is the final illusion. The family and friends file past the open casket for a last look. They retain what the funeral profession refers to as a "memory picture."

Then the sacrifice: It is all consigned to the earth or to the flames. It is gone. It becomes a bronze tablet lying flat amidst the blades of freshly mowed grass, while underneath, despite the preservatives, despite the concrete grave liner, the bronze and the constant talk of "protection," it all very quickly rots.

Or it becomes ashes. A pamphlet from another funeral home says: "Flame accomplishes in a brief time what interment takes years to accomplish, but the end result is essentially the same."

After cremation there is nothing left but a few large fragments of bone. The casket is completely gone except for the hardware. "I've got a barrelful of the pieces I could show you."

Mr. Case takes you out to the garage. But the hearses and the limousines are parked outside, the garage full of caskets temporarily moved out of the sample display room while the carpet is being shampooed. The crematory is in one corner. It resembles a garden toolshed, the sides of corrugated sheet metal painted green and white. A cremation costs $75. Case does an average of one per day, and he can do as many as five. The process takes two hours. There is a thirty-minute "burn" period, followed by one and a half hours of controlled heat that reduces everything to ashes. Then there is a half hour cooling period. Up to another hour may be necessary if the body is very large.

The door has safety controls that automatically turn off the flames when it is opened. There is an observation port. After peering inside, Mr. Case opens the door. "There's one in there now. It's all ready to go." Go ahead and look. Inside the fire-brick-lined combustion chamber there is a casket.

He points to the jets at the top and the bottom, fed by a 500-gallon tank of propane gas—about a month's supply of fuel—that is buried underground. The gas burns at 1,800 degrees under forced air. Beside the door are a series of controls and knobs and gauges much as you have on your kitchen oven. One is marked "Master Timer," another "Temperature."

Leaning against the garage wall is a long, heavy bar with a ring on one end, a heavy crosspiece on the other. This is the rake for dragging out the residue of bone. Next to the rake is a loose stack of blackened and twisted pieces of metal, the hinges, handles and corner pieces remaining from the caskets, light-gauge sheet metal that was originally covered with a very thin decorative plating. The pieces cannot be salvaged as junk because the alloys are gone. They load up a truck periodically and take it all out to the county dump.

From the shelves in a storage closet on the other side of the garage Mr. Case takes down several packages wrapped in brown paper and marked in black crayon with a model number and the style. He rips off the wrappers to show the different types of urns, some of bronze-plated steel, others of solid bronze. He invites you to feel the difference in weight. Prices vary from $50 to $100, but he doesn't carry some of the more elaborate and ornate models, like the replica of a large bronze Bible. Most of them are about the size of a kitchen sugar can, but the ashes fill only about half of the urn—like the cookie and cereal boxes in the supermarkets that are never more than half full. The rest of the space is packed with cotton. Then Mr. Case unwraps a very small urn about the size and shape of a peanut can. It is for babies. It is the "cherub" model.

Go into the display room, the pale-green carpet showing the clean rectangles where the caskets have been resting between the dirty corridors of accumulated footprints. Back in the garage, you can look at a few samples. By coincidence, the cheapest casket is lying next to the most expensive—gray moleskin cloth stretched over cheap wood next to solid bronze, $595 next to $5,000. Against a far wall, under some loose odds and ends, is a stack of three plain wooden boxes without paint or ornaments. These are used for the occasional no-view, no-service cremation.

In a small open space nearby is another box. It is plain, made of dark, gleaming, oiled oak. Without really seeing it, your mind numbed by the afternoon's input of information, you think of what a gorgeous chest it would make for linen. And then you see the wooden railing fastened to the side. And then the Star of David carved on the top. Mr. Case is still moving quickly, still talking and explaining. The casket has been made according to Jewish tradition—that is, entirely of wood, without nails.

"This is another one they sent up from Miami. We'll do it tonight."

He reaches over and raises the lid. There is a man inside. He is wearing a white satin yarmulka, the traditional skull cap. There is powder on his face. His lips are serene. His eyes are closed.

Leave. Sit in the car a few minutes. Try to think. Remember that Mr. Case said they do the cremations at night because of the heat factor. Later he said it was because there was less personnel activity. But he also mentioned the importance of having the crematory controls properly adjusted, and he referred to the heavy black smoke that would result if they weren't. Behind the Baird-Case funeral home is an apartment building. In front of it is U.S. 1, the main federal highway.

And you wonder if the neighboring tenants ever notice the thin heat waves outside their windows that sometimes waver skyward, outlined against the moon rising up from the nearby beach, hazing the swiftly dazzling line of headlights rushing north and south. And do they ever wonder about what is being converted into vapor out there in the night? What figments burn beside that frantic avenue of moving traffic, what flesh, what clothing, what chemicals and craftsmanship? What pain and passion, humor, anger, fear and hope? What hard, cold residue of love?

He was well over sixty. On the open desk calendar was a notation: "The Day Margaret Died." It remained untouched. Exactly one year later, on March 15th, he called the funeral home where he had already made prearrangements. When asked the name of the deceased, he answered:

"Me. This is a suicide. Please come pick up my body."

Then he called the police, walked into the bathroom, and blew his head off with a shotgun.

16 The black section of Bartow has narrow streets, overgrown yards, roofs of tar paper, and rusting galvanized iron. Two blocks east of the railroad tracks is a small, square building, the walls made of cement blocks, the joints crooked, the mortar squeezed out in uneven globs, the corners out of plumb. The roof is flat and has no eaves. The sash windows are closed and dirty, protected by galvanized wire mesh. There is a red, white and blue park bench out in front. There is a sandy path instead of a sidewalk. On one of the windows hangs a flaky sign, sun-faded and barely legible: CHARLIE SMITH—SOFT DRINKS—CANDY BARS. The screen door sags, misshapen and padlocked.

At the next corner is a row of small cabins built of limestone rocks. Four black Muslim women sit on the first splintered, unpainted porch, dressed in white habits, their feet bare, their faces impassive, one holding up a shepherd's staff with a bird carved on top of the crook.

A fifth woman in an ordinary dress calls out, "He ain't home. They all gone on up to Kentucky."

The Muslim ladies say nothing, indicating nothing, moving not at all, sitting on their benches and chairs and looking out over the narrow, quiet street, the yards sandy and without lawns, a clump of bromeliads growing at the base of a nearby oak tree.

"He be back sometime. Next week."

And they sit and they wait and they think about their neighbor, Charlie Smith, the oldest person in the United States. On the Fourth of July he will be 131 years old.

He was born in 1842 and was kidnapped in Liberia when he was twelve years old, lured aboard a sailing ship by a white man who promised to show him the corn-fritter trees that grew in America. He was sold at a slave auction in New Orleans to a rancher from Texas named Charlie Smith, who adopted him, raised him as an equal to his five other children, and gave him his own name. There is on record a New Orleans bill of sale for a twelve-year-old slave, dated 1854. The Social Security office has accepted this as proof of his age.

But as a matter of dependable, verifiable record, no one, anywhere in the world, has ever lived to be 114. The oldest authenticated American died at 112. During the entire 1,000-year history of the British nobility, only one peer ever lived to be 100. The oldest British commoner died at 111. In Sweden, where there is a detailed official investigation into every claim of extreme longevity, no Swede has ever been proven to have lived beyond 110.

In Russia there is a man who says he is 167, and the

government claims nearly 600 Russians over 120. These people, however, were born under the Czar, when it was common for a man to assume the identity of an older man to escape military service.

Accurate birth records are a recent thing, and no one can be really sure. But it is known that very old people tend to exaggerate their age, and this tendency increases in illiterate regions where records are also undependable or nonexistent. Memories become weak. Identities are blurred. Favorite stories become more comfortable and finally real. The histories and the legends of others become confused and then appropriated for themselves.

It was raining and sticky hot. A faint voice finally answered from behind the raw plywood partition that divided the store.

"Wait till ah gits dere!"

And then he came hobbling out, his back stiff and bent forward at the waist. He was wearing socks, a dark-blue sweater buttoned all the way up, a black bow tie, and a pink-checked dress shirt. His pants and jockey shorts were down over his hips as he fumbled with the tail of his shirt and muttered, "Sit down. Sit down. Ah'm tryin' to go to de toilet."

He turned and shuffled back, flashing a view of the oldest, possibly the blackest and certainly one of the skinniest asses in the country.

A portable TV was showing a baseball game. It was new, two red ribbons still attached to the casing. One wall of the room was decorated with framed documents and signs. A battered sofa with a dirty cover was in the middle of the room facing the front door. On display were several framed certificates propped up against the back rest. He had been made a Kentucky Colonel. He was an honorary captain of the riverboat *Belle of Louisville*. He had been honored by the cities of Gardena and Los Angeles and by the Kennedy Space Center.

There was an old worn carpet on the concrete floor. A disconnected gas range was in one corner, a dilapidated sofa torn and rotting in another corner, a rusting Nehi cold-drink box in the third corner next to an old refrigerator that ran with a loud motor. There were piles of junk, stacks of wooden cases, dirty empty bottles, a handful of new, unsharpened pencils in a paper cup, red paper flowers, and several old wooden folding chairs. At the door was a galvanized garbage can.

He came in and sat down on the open end of his trophy sofa. But he didn't understand the word, nor did he grasp the concept of "retired."

"Ah ain't—ah ain't done no woik in—ah don' reggen in a hunnerd years. Ah'm a state man. De state take keer o' me. Ah work for de state."

"What did you do when you worked for the state?"

"Go anywhere dey tell me to go an' do. All dis heah."

He turned his head and waved a hand loosely toward the wall behind him bearing its testimonials of distinction.

"An' all dat. All over. Different states. Check 'em. Doctors. Lawyers. An' all dat. High sheriff. Polices. Dat's mah job."

"What kind of work did you do before?"

"Anything dey tell me to do. Ah'm de man went an' got de man what killed de Presi-dent. Me an' Billy de

Kid. Went an' got Git-tah. And Git-tah killed de President. Garfield. His home was in Long Branch, Missouri. Me an' Billy started over dere to git 'im for five hunnerd dolla' reward."

"Do you remember much about the war with Cuba? Tampa was the big town for that war. Were there a lot of soldiers around?"

"Yeah. Dem people dere in Tampa den. What dey call. Dey was fightin' de war in Cuba. Dey's Spaniards. And Cubans. Dey was fightin' de war. Ah stay out dere at dat turpentine still. Right in de woods. For a turpentine man name Pettaway."

"Teddy Roosevelt was President then, wasn't he?"

"Name Pettaway."

"Teddy Roosevelt. Wasn't he the President then?"

"Who?"

"Teddy Roosevelt."

"Roosevelt? Yeah. Ah was known about him. De Presidents. Ah known about de Presi-dents. All—ah'm de man. Me an' Billy de Kid. Went an' got de man. Killed. Went an' got Garfield."

A truck roared up the street outside.

"Git-tah killed Garfield. He was de Presi-dent. Ah was in Texas den. Ah was raised in Texas. Now mah movies name. Mah movies name. Is Trigger Kid. Anybody goin' in de movies pitchers den or now. Dey gi' you a movies name. Man raised me put me in on de movies pitchers. Ah'm a movies player."

"Did you make many movies?"

"Mah name. Movies name. Is Trigger Kid. An' Billy de Kid. He's a white fella. He. Me an' Billy de Kid. Went an' got de man. Killed. Went an' got dat Gittah. Git-tah

killed de Presi-dent. His home is Long Branch, Missouri.
He was born and raised dere. We went over dere to git
fer five hunnerd dolla' reward. People in dat state kill
'im. Keep 'em from gittin' it. An' dey sont me. An' Billy
de Kid. Went over dere. Dey say. 'An' sen' de Kids dere.'
Trigger Kid an' Billy de Kid. See? Dere where we at. An'
dere was five hunnerd dolla' reward."

"Did you catch them and turn them in?"

"Yeah. We got 'em."

"Where did you bring them to?"

"Don' ask so many questions. Ah'm tryin' to tell yuh."

"Oh. I'm sorry."

It went on—the repetitions, the pauses, the unintelli-
gible mutterings, his voice weak and failing. He would
fumble in a pack of Pall Malls with his big-knuckled
fingers, light up still another smoke, let the ashes fall on
the sofa, the carpet, his own socks and feet, only occasionally remembering the empty sardine-can ashtray on
the rusty old metal folding chair beside him. He fondled
the big button on his sweater, a souvenir of the Apollo
XVII moon shot which he witnessed as a guest of the
government. He claimed it was his state badge. He was
the only one allowed to wear it, colored or white, his grin
wide and pleasant, a slight bulge in his lower left lip
where the yellow and brown stump of one tooth still
remained.

He didn't remember much about Africa, being only a
boy when he left.

"It like countin' money. Benesenka. Whut benesenka
mean?"

"I have no idea. Is that the Liberian language?"

"Ah say. Whut it mean? Whut does benesenka mean?"

"I don't know."

"Whut shitawa mean?"

"I don't know. I have no idea. What does it mean?"

"Benesenka. Shitawa. Benesenka. Dat's a nickel. Benesenka shitawa. Dat's a quarter. In other states. Not de
United States now. Dat's a quarter in Africa. Benesenka
shitawa is a quarter. Benesenka by itself. Dat's a nickel."

"Can you remember any other African?"

"Ah tole yuh, didn't ah? Ain't ah tellin' yuh now?
Good Gawd. Ah'm tellin' yuh whut it mean in Africa.
Benesenka. Dat's a nickel. In Africa. Benesenka shitawa
is a quarter in Africa. Dat's de way yuh count your
money in Africa, mister."

He lit another cigarette and repeated old man Smith's
advice about never running out of basic needs, about
paying your bills but never letting yourself go broke.

"Ah'm de oldes' person now livin' in de Newnited
States."

He fumbled in a worn leather folder on the sofa, pull-
ing out a copy of Robert Ripley's column "Believe It or
Not" published in 1955. At that time Charlie Smith was
picking oranges in Winter Haven. There was a drawing
of him and also of a man named Pereira. Charlie was
brought to a hospital in Denver for a medical study,
where he met Pereira, who had been discovered in the
Andes Mountains of Colombia by a Ripley expedition.

"Dis man daid since den. He was older'n ah was. Ah
was 113 when me an' him met. And he was 166. But he
died since den. Me an' him met. An' dat throwed to me
den to be de oldest person."

"How do you figure you got to be so old?"

"Well. By Gawd. Gawd he'p."

"Did you take special care of yourself?"

"Ah woiks. Ah woiks jes like other people. Doin' Gawd's thing. Was brought me from Africa. De colored people always did hate me. An ah' wa'n't but twelve year old. An' dey wanted to throw me off. De boat."

"Do you see a doctor often? How is your health?"

"Oh. Ah feels real bad. Been feelin' bad. Right now. Ah feels bad. Many days dat ah don' straighten out mah bed. Gits tired. Walkin' roun' de bed. Gits tired and hafta rest. Ah don' hurt nowhere. Jes feels bad."

"Do you take anything for it?"

"Naw. Jes some li'l ole pills. Dey he'p mah feelin's. Da's all. Ah don' hurt nowhere."

He lit up another cigarette.

"Oh, yeah. Ah drink whiskey. Fust thing ah do ever' mornin' when ah git up. If ah got it. Take me a BC an' a drink. It don't cure me, but it jes he'ps mah feelin's."

"Do you eat very much?"

"Naw. Some days ah don' eat nothin'. Ah don' git hongry nuff to eat. Ah drink milk. Oranges. Ah don't eat much cooked rations. Ah eat mos'ly. Candy. Or stuff like dat. Jes custard pie. Somethin' sweet. Somethin' like dat.

"Do you think about dying much ever? How long do you think you're going to live?"

"Oh. Ah don' know. Ah don't know nothin' about all dat. Ah cain't tell nothin' about how long ah'm gonna live."

"Do you believe in heaven?"

"Yeah. Ah believe in heaven. Dere's a heaven some-where. Dere's some private place somewhere in de worl'. But ah don' know where 'tis. You don' know where 'tis. Ain' nobody on earth knows where 'tis. Say. 'Heaven.'

Dat whut dey say. But dey don' know where heaven is at. Man. De only thing. Shoot a rocket up. Dey brought de paper here to me. 'Bout a year ago. You mighta read dat in de paper. Say dey brought rocks back. De man went to de moon. Come back he brought rocks. Dey brought de paper. Had dat in de paper. An ah said if dey brought rocks back, ah said dey carry 'em up dere wit' 'em. Ah say, 'Dere ain' no way. Whut dey stop in de air? Whut dey—gone git out an' walk? An' got rocks? In de air? Ah say, 'No. Ah don' believe dat.' Well. Ah di'n't. An' don't believe it yet. So dat last time dey went up, de Presi-dent require me to be over dere when dey shoot you up to de moon. De Presi-dent an' de Gov'nor require an' say dey want me to have me over dere. In Miami. An' when dey come back soon dey gonna see de man. Ole man Charlie Smith. De oldes' person in de worl'. Dey wanna see 'im."

On the wall was a calendar from the Independent Life and Accident Insurance Company. There was a photograph and the legend "Americans in Space." Three cowboy hats were stacked together in a pile. There was a framed astronaut shoulder patch from the Apollo XVII mission. There was a bare bulb hanging on a wire, a metal clothes hanger attached to the pull string. A box of Tide was on the gas range, a pile of Baby Ruth boxes, one Ex-Lax box, a plastic pitcher, a dusty glass light fixture, a razor and shaving brush in a cup. On the rusted Nehi cold-drink box was an empty sardine can and three oranges.

More. There was more about Sunday school and everyday school in Liberia, where he was taught about the world turning on its axle. He didn't believe that lie either. He got a ladder and some nails and some rope and tied the porch of his house to a tree, telling his mother how he was going to disprove all that nonsense about sun-in-the-east-and-sun-in-the-west. And that stuff about the devil. And getting rocks out of the air. And hell. But this is hell right here.

"When you die you ain't got to go nowhere. You already in hell."

He believed some parts of the Bible but not all of it. No one had any real idea of what God was going to do. People are always believing what they read. Charlie himself never even bothered to learn. Everybody believes to this day what the Scriptures say about Lincoln freeing the slaves. But none of this is true. He knew because he was there. What really happened was this: The Northern white folks also bought slaves, but because the colored people couldn't stand the cold weather they were left in the South in care of the Southern white folks. But then the Southerners began to mistreat the Northerners' slaves and they got mad. They told the Southerners they had to free their own slaves. They wouldn't do it, so there was a war. Because the colored ladies were forced into birthing children for the Southern white folks. And that's why Louisiana was given to the colored people so it could be their very own territory. Which is why the Northerners were called "Yankees."

But Charlie was never in the Army himself. He already had a job. He was a state man. He and Billy the Kid had to get Gittah. The man who killed the President. He had a badge. No one else was allowed to wear it.

(President Garfield was assassinated in 1881, the same year Billy the Kid was killed. The assassin was caught on the scene in Washington, D.C., and hanged a year later. His name was Charles Julius Guiteau.)

Charlie Smith groped and fumbled with a photograph album. Very slowly he produced a page out of some history book enclosed in plastic. And there were the pictures of Billy the Kid and Jesse James and his nineteen-year-old son. And they had to go through the Hookin' Bulls Ranch. But they didn't need those passes demanded by the cowboys. They just shot off the locks with their .45s and challenged the foreman. Off and on. Off your horse and on the ground. Or you will be too wet to plow. Charlie's red bandanna was thrown on the ground in challenge. It was the signal. It was his flag. And when they returned from the Sandy Desert back to the United States, he and Billy the Kid went to work for Jesse James. They saw his newborn son a week before he did himself.

And then with a thin, quavering voice, Charlie Smith sang the same lullaby that Jesse James crooned to his baby over a hundred years ago. Holding out his emaciated arms, he gently rocked from side to side.

"Hush, hush, don't you cry. You gonna be a millionaire before you die."

Trigger Kid. That was his movies name. Just like Billy the Kid. But the name his momma gave him was Mitchell Watkins. She let him go down to the boat landing. He had never seen a white man. So she said, all right. He could go.

* * *

She was fifty-two. She got mad when her husband came home late, followed him into the bathroom with a .22-caliber automatic pistol and shot him six times. She went to the front door to tell the alarmed neighbors what she had done. They called the police. She went into the bedroom. Meanwhile, her husband had only pretended to be dead. He ran out the back door, got a .22 rifle out of the car, came back in and killed her with one shot.

* * *

She was eighty-two. She sang gypsy songs and gave a command performance for the Czar in 1908. They asked for an encore. She became a court favorite. When Rasputin tried to seduce her, using force, she stuck a small knife into his chest. She came to New York and married a Russian prince. They had two daughters, but one of them disappeared. They came to Florida. At eighty she was widowed. She got sick. Her other daughter came down to take care of her. But her son-in-law hired a Marine for $1,500, a round-trip airplane ticket, and $70 for expenses to murder both of them. The Marine couldn't go through with it. They were too nice. He surrendered two knives and a pair of leather gloves. Her son-in-law was arrested. He had once been elected "Top Pop" in a Father's Day contest.

He was sixty-three. He crawled under a table in an abandoned downtown building to sleep. Early in the morning a demolition crew arrived. He woke up with the walls collapsing all around him, crying and screaming as he ran out in the street. He was charged with public drunkenness and spent the next night in jail.

* * *

17 One of the auctioneers blocked the door against the three hippies, growling his gruff attempt to be convincingly tough. "This is a private sale. I'm telling you." But then he stepped aside, opening the door as he muttered, "What are you gonna do? First we used to let 'em in. Now they don't wanna wear shoes even."

The evening started with a demonstration of the door prizes that were going to be given away later. A tall, thin young man with a very low brow and a smirk that never left his mouth was showing off the various gadgets and toys, like the penny bank and the electronic dog. He resembled one of the three older brothers, the proprietors, who all wore fashionable suits with wide lapels and ties in bright, pastel colors. Their expressions were deadpan, bored, and very professional.

It began with a little routine. The auctioneer was impeccably dressed, his shoulders braced, posture perfect, voice forceful, well modulated and hypnotic. With long, thoughtful pauses, a hint of introspection that made him all the more convincing, he introduced the proceedings.

"We will not insult your intelligence and say we do not make a profit. We are liquidators. We buy estates and we deal with some of the biggest banks in the country."

He waved his hand at the packed collection of brand-new, pseudo-antique junk, the porcelain dogs, cats, elephants and ballet dancers, the assembly-line-produced paintings of shepherdesses, fishing boats and angelic children, the figurines, the Oriental rugs, vases, chandeliers, coffee tables and lamps. Then he held up a figurine with a delicate reverence.

"You know what this is?"

"Bisque" came the answer.

"Right. Know what it means?"

"Half baked," sang the audience.

"Right. What sharp people we got here tonight. Like me. I'm half baked too. I got a wife and four chairs."

The flimflam commenced. With bored, mechanical motions, the assistants moved up and down the aisles, showing the wares. Blatantly, the young, skinny, low-brow cynic with the smirk made bids himself to keep things going, muttering out of the side of his mouth, to raise the bids or to start them off. But if the price was really right the auctioneer coolly awarded the prize to the bidder without any further charade. None of this going-once, going-twice stuff. It was yours.

And so it went—glass paperweights, cookie-jar sets, end tables, Louis any-number-you-likes. A large soup tureen covered with glazed roses and carrots went for $30. A shill went up the aisle wearing ten rings on ten fingers, showing them off. A motorcycle roared by just outside. The auctioneer shrugged with a prolonged, compound grimace that got a snicker from the audience. To demonstrate the color and the sparkle of a lamp hung with crystal pendants, the overhead lights were briefly turned off.

They sat there and gawked. They whispered and consulted. They fidgeted and calculated and worried. An old woman had two plastic catleyas in her hair. Another had a real corsage on her breast. Her hair was blue. A woman sitting in front of you had a beehive hairdo, iron gray, augmented by a thick fall. Her false eyelashes were incredibly long, her skin a very deep tan. All around were $5 Sears, Roebuck pleated slacks, cheap shoes with colored ankle socks that had no elastic, Bermuda shorts, McCrory's costume jewelry, muu-muus, wrinkles and fat. But there was also the agitation of a fever gradually rising, the competition, the acquisition, the thrill of a gamble, a fight, the thirst for a victory. It was the only possible place where a milkman, a moonshiner and a Mafioso could meet together in equal awe.

And so it went—pandas in fake fur, monkeys in glazed clay. A silver service was auctioned off, but this was not the night. No one seemed to notice that one of the shills himself apparently bought it for only $80. You were treated to lengthy descriptions of the high quality of the goods being offered. It was all *"porcelaine de Paris"* and *"Capa di Monte,"* Belfast linen and Dresden china and Sterling silver. You kept hearing about the famous "hallmarks" and the traditional "kiln marks." One woman in front bought several knickknacks, bidding very anxiously, lost in the thrill of the competition but then nervously worried and whispering to her husband, seeking the reassurance that she really and truly had made a terrific bargain.

When a bid was successful you gave the auctioneer your initials, which were written on a slip of paper. Later you claimed your object at the cashier's desk. The auctioneer was familiar with several people in the crowd. Regulars. He seemed to know their initials without asking.

And then several hippies looked through the plate-glass window. They were the Easter freaks who invade Ft. Lauderdale's beach every year, all acne and bare bellies and denim shirts, beads and bangles, dirty feet, long and greasy hair, bib overalls and hobo hats. Fascinated, they pressed close to the glass, peering inside at this intense ritual. But the old-timers all turned their heads and glared at them, the scowling, hard-jawed, tight-lipped faces of Buffalo and Independence, Portland and Des Moines. They frowned back at these mocking barbarians through the reflections and the lights and the images of their Chinese "ivory" and their French "period" pieces, the crystal and lace, the tapestry, the marble, the gilt, the rhinestones, their wrinkled features defiant through the shimmering images of their treasures.

She was twenty-one. She enrolled in a course called "philosophy of death." As part of her class project she persuaded a funeral director to let her lie in a coffin. They closed the lid and left her alone for an hour and a half.

He was thirty-five. He was a health addict, never smoked and never drank. His business had been robbed of $50,000 worth of merchandise. He had no insurance. A former girlfriend and partner accused him of embezzling $8,000. He was already an ex-convict. In the middle of winter he went scuba diving in freezing water wearing a thick neoprene suit. He was an expert diver, but he didn't come up. The police dragged the bottom. His wife went hysterical. But three weeks later he called her up. He was in Miami Beach. He grew a beard, acquired false identification, added ten years to his age, traveled to New Orleans and *to Rio de Janeiro, remarried his wife under his new name, worked hard, became a very successful professional diver, and took out a life-insurance policy. Three years later he went with a boatload of tourists to the Bahamas on a diving expedition. A storm came up. Two other divers got in trouble but were rescued. He disappeared. The radio wouldn't work. It started to rain heavily. A Coast Guard plane, a cutter and two helicopters helped the charter boat search the area for two days. They were assisted by another plane, another helicopter and three ships. His body was never found. The insurance company went to court. The jury denied death benefits to his wife.*

18 Charlie Brick's island was only a spoil bank, a few mangrove trees and a few Australian pines growing in the sand and rocks dredged up by the Army Corps of Engineers when they sucked out a twelve-foot channel for barges and yachts. His ocean was really the Indian River, which is really a lagoon, a narrow strip of natural salt water between the mainland and the beach offshore. Fishermen, tourists, newspaper reporters, hippies, yachtsmen, photographers, everybody stopped by at Seven Pine Shoal. Every year they gathered in his shack to celebrate his birthday. He grinned and posed for pictures, wearing his gilt crown of cardboard. He was blue-eyed and toothless and eighty-three.

He was king of the island. He ran naked with his dog over his one-and-a-half-acre domain, his long blond-and-white beard curling in the wind. He had a pet pigeon, and he had a flock of arracauna chickens, jungle birds that looked like ordinary fighting cocks except that these laid colored eggs, either pink ones or blue ones or green ones. He also had a guest registration book and three Christmas cards from President Nixon.

He lived there for twelve years. He and Duke enjoyed nature in the raw, barking at seagulls, conning the tourists, pooping at the end of the sandbar at low tide. All they needed was that $174 every month from Social Security.

But within four months he was living in a low-rent housing-authority apartment building for the elderly. Duke was dead and buried on the island. Charlie had been in and out of the hospital with the flu. He padded around in wool socks and jockey shorts, the windows sealed and the air stifling. He was cooking a pot of stew in the kitchen. The last dairy bill was taped to the refrigerator door. Inside were six quarts of ice cream.

He hauled out a cardboard box full of old newspaper articles that had been written about him, most of them reprints of the same AP wire-service story. On a raw plywood table was a stack of racing forms. He was determined to develop a system to beat the horses. He had television, a card table, a few chairs. The stew simmered. The kitchen was scattered with dirty dishes and stained newspapers. No. He was never going back to the island. He had already sold his shack. The thing was, to live out there in comfort required hauling out these tanks of butane gas in a boat for the stove and the oven and the refrigerator. And they weighed thirty or forty pounds. He just couldn't handle them anymore.

19 Orvil Azbell is a barber, a nervous, quick-moving man, very much involved with other people. His business card advertises: "Free information about love, marriage, weather, baseball, hunting, fishing, politics and football." And down at the bottom: "We also cut hair." About once a month Orvil travels to several nursing homes, going up in the evening to plug a portable box into an outlet. It operates electric clippers and vacuums up the hair at the same time.

At the Manor Pines Convalescent Home he cuts the hair of Ed Hall, a World War II bomber pilot who suffers from multiple sclerosis and is confined to a wheelchair. He has been here four and a half years. When Orvil is finished, he pushes the wheelchair in front of the wall mirror. Ed Hall asks for just a little bit more off the left. Disguising his chagrin, Orvil replugs the machine, deftly touching the indicated spot. He waits, wondering, standing by. Mr. Hall cocks his head, examining the reflection of his closely cropped, gray hair that narrowly fringes the bald center. He asks for just a little more off the back.

Ed Hall's job in the Army Air Corps was training the crews of the radar ships that guided the bombing fleets through the clouds and mists over Germany. He saw no combat himself. But occasionally he would have trouble with his leg. After a fast game of handball it would sometimes drag. The flight surgeons always had him walk up and down the corridors and said there was nothing wrong with him. But they did enter it into the record, which is why Ed Hall now gets a government pension for a service-incurred disability. He gets another pension from Social Security and still another from the insurance company for which he worked as a salesman.

Multiple sclerosis is one of those medical mysteries. How it happens is totally unknown, and no two cases are ever quite the same. After his separation from the service, Captain Hall went home to Connecticut, where he went into the insurance field. But after spending four winters in Florida, he suffered from the cold and soon began using a cane. It was the cold weather that made him go back to Florida permanently, even though he had to start his insurance business all over again.

For twelve years he gradually became worse, and then, after a bad general infection, he was confined to a wheelchair. He knew about the regressive steps of his disease and always planned ahead, using hand controls on his automobile before they were really necessary and having his new house designed specifically for wheelchair use.

His left arm atrophied, then his hand. In 1965 the disease began to affect his right side. He had to give up driving. He had to retire. He and his wife agreed that they would never burden their children. She checked out the various convalescent homes in the area. They sold their house, and she moved into a rented duplex. Ed Hall entered Manor Pines in September 1967. His wife committed suicide eight months later.

His voice was painfully slow and very, very soft. He answered briefly, initiating nothing. And nothing could inspire any intensity. But he did testify about his experiences at Manor Pines. He said they do a real good job. Everybody griped about the food, just like in the Army, but he had no complaints. There was an organ in the home, and every Sunday there were volunteer lay preachers who came in to conduct services. The management in some way recognized every religious holiday, no matter what kind. He went out for dinner occasionally, his daughter, who lived in Hollywood, picking him up. Once a week a friend took him to lunch at the Lions Club.

After his wife died, his two married daughters both wanted him to come live with them. But he refused.

"It wouldn't be good for them. It wouldn't be right."

They did convince him, however, that he should have a private room. It was large and comfortable and air-conditioned, the colors all soft beiges and tans. It cost him $26.50 per day, including meals and twenty-four-hour nursing care. He had two calendars on the walls. There were color photographs of his daughters' weddings. There was a plaque depicting two hands folded in prayer with an inscription underneath, "More things are wrought by prayer than the world dreams of." There was another plaque on another wall, an award he won as "outstanding Lion of the year." He had served a term as executive secretary while already in a wheelchair. There was a vase of plastic yellow roses on the dresser. There were photographs, a radio, a small color TV set, a tape player. There was a Bible, a stack of *Reader's Digests*, a miniature flag, a book titled *How to Get Along with Black People*. There was a frame and a trapeze at the head of his bed. On the bureau and on the window sill were a statuette of praying hands, a picture of Christ, a miniature hourglass, a beer stein, a pair of glasses with heavy black frames. An American flag decal was on the window pane.

With obvious difficulty, he shifted his left leg up and down from the foot rest. He wore a brace on that leg. He was dressed in a short-sleeve shirt of raspberry pink and a tan sleeveless sweater. His slacks were bright blue. His posture was slumped. He always held his bad left hand with his right one. The next day would be his birthday. He would be fifty-five.

He felt content. "If you ever feel sorry for yourself, I recommend that you go to a VA hospital and look at some cases. For that matter, check any emergency room." Besides, he still looked forward to getting well again, convinced he would be, but not through medical science.

"I believe in miracle healings. I really do. They can be very sudden. Not just overnight. Like. Right now."

Softly and slowly, he said it was hard to explain. He didn't think he was a crackpot. It had to be because of God. After all, Satan had a lot to do with his being where he was. He believed there was a force in the world that was satanic, just as he believed in the hereafter and in the Bible. Mr. Hall had no specific plans beyond his healing. He wanted to become active, to work and to somehow help other people. But he had always believed that an insurance salesman helps people if he is sincere and if he is competent. He himself had hundreds of clients who were also friends.

He never despaired while waiting for his miracle. He grew silent for a long moment and then quietly murmured, "I know that it's possible."

He was never bored. He corresponded frequently with an aunt who was 94 1/2, with his mother-in-law, with a cousin and his two daughters. He read. He had music, his TV and his visitors.

"There are prophecies in the Book of Revelations which foretell all the bad things happening in this country today. We are going down. We have more crime. We have kids who are the products of Dr. Spock's permissiveness. But that is only a partial explanation because permissiveness is not world-wide as is the trend toward decadence. It is lack of religious faith. The Communists are strong anti-Christs, not like the democracies of the world. But nothing can be done about it. It is almost as bad as Sodom and Gomorrah at the time of the ark."

Mr. Hall thought the Second Coming of Christ might be very near. But he wasn't sure. He thought the Communist threat was all part of the forces of evil. Also the drugs. And the promiscuity. He wasn't sure if the Communists started the drug craze or simply took advantage of it. Maybe that too was part of the Marxist plan. He didn't know.

The space program could lead to good things. The

radar research during World War II resulted in the mass production of cathode ray tubes, which helped the development of television. Technology was like a snowball rolling down a hill. Nothing could stop it. But we were improving materially and degenerating spiritually. There were still flashes of good news. A spiritual reawakening was occurring all over the world. We had the Jesus People, proven to be the only answer to drug addiction. And yet, we were decaying.

The sexual revolution? That was all part of it. The Bible said all this would lead to the Second Coming. There was bound to be a big explosion, especially in the Middle East. How far could we go? Who could say? In the old days of the Bible they had the ark. It had been found to be a fact of life. They located its remains frozen on the top of Mt. Ararat in Turkey. They found the timbers and checked their age. A rescue party tried to get in to get more wood for tests and measurements. But the Russians wouldn't let them into the country.

Russians? In Turkey? There was a pause and then a quiet, almost breathless murmur.

"Communists."

He was seventy-nine. He was baby-sitting for his eight-year-old godson. He let him play with his .22 pistol and showed him how to clean it. Later, he ordered the boy inside the house. The boy became angry, got the pistol and shot his godfather, who was treated at the hospital and released the same day. Six days later he returned to complain that the wound in his head was not healing. And then he died. The boy was arrested and charged with murder.

✳   ✳   ✳

20 It is ten o'clock. The clerks and secretaries and switchboard operators have already been working for an hour, handling the paperwork of previous trading sessions. The customer's men are ready at their desks, neat and cool in their ties and suits and shined shoes. The boardroom regulars are sitting in the rows of theater seats, waiting, fidgeting, staring up at the long rectangular blank space high up on the wall. And then it begins to move, teleprinted letters and numbers followed by the swift succession of symbols that indicate the stock, the number of shares and the price.

—GOOD MORNING—MARKET OPEN—

IBM 1500s 331½ T 1200s 48¼ NOM 7s 35⅛ SSC 3s 29⅝

A customer's man is on the phone. He writes down an order to sell one hundred shares of XYZ. Quickly, he makes a series of marks and numbers in the appropriate spaces on the order blank. He asks the customer at what price he should sell it. The customer says, sell it at the high for the day. Very slowly and very patiently the customer's man tries to explain that no one will know the high for the day until the day is over.

Across the aisle another account executive slides open a drawer, takes out a can of peanuts, leans back in his chair and reads the latest Argus report. On his desk is a small statuette of a bull. It is made of glass.

Another panel up on the board shows a projection of the news tape. As the teletype is activated, the words are miraculously written on the wall:

NATIONAL DIVERSIFIED INDUSTRIES SAID IT PLANS TO DISTRIBUTE AND MARKET DOLLY MADISON PRODUCTS THROUGH ITS AZALEA OPERATIONS IN THE SOUTH AND TO SELL ITS AZALEA MEAT PRODUCTS THROUGH—

One old man sits in a slouch, his feet propped up on the seat in front of him, his ankles crossed, his white buckskin loafers gleaming. He is a retired mailman and he comes in occasionally to spend a few hours. Beside him sits a toothless old geezer with a sharp beak of a nose and large liver blotches on his face. He is wearing a wrinkled old hound's-tooth jacket, seersucker shorts, a battered straw hat, ankle-length red socks and dilapidated, worn-out loafers. He watches the tape every day. Everybody in the boardroom knows him. He is worth about seven million dollars.

The cigar smoke is thicker. The manager comes out of his glass-walled office. He has rumpled gray hair and a rumpled gray suit. He bends over to talk to Mr. Jones, a grizzled old man who always sits in the same seat in the back row with an old golf cap on his head cocked at an angle. A revolutionary group has just staged a political coup in Libya. Occidental Petroleum has a large percentage of its assets in the oil fields of Libya. Mr. Jones has a large percentage of his assets in Occidental Petroleum. The stock has been falling, sharply. The manager whispers, his forehead wrinkled as his eyes look upward, never leaving the tape. There is a strangled cry from Mr. Jones as he waves his arm, his gesture floundering in a desperate wave for something to grab, to hold onto.

"This is just emotional. That's all it is."

The manager straightens up, embarrassed. His eyes still watching the tape, he moves up the carpeted aisle and goes back to his office.

$$^{SPS}_{5S}\ 12\tfrac{1}{4}\ \tfrac{1}{4}\ ^{CLL}_{26\tfrac{1}{4}}\ .2S\tfrac{1}{4}\ ^{LNC}pr_{5S}\ 81^{PBI}_{36}{}^{HMD}_{12\tfrac{1}{8}}\ ^{GM}_{74}$$

The regulars go out for coffee and they go to the john. They make phone calls. They sit without moving, hunched, sprawled, clutching their chart books, their news releases, their latest copy of some market advisory service, their notebooks.

"Did you see that block of IBM go through just then? One thousand shares at 338. That was a gap up from 337 on volume. I just saw it. I wonder what's going on?"

BROKERS ATTRIBUTE THE MARKET-S LETHARGY IN PART TO DISAPPOINTMENT THERE WAS NO FOLLOW-THROUGH ·YESTERDAY TO LAST WEEK-S RALLY—THEY ADD THAT SOME HESITATION CONTINUES TO STEM FROM THE OUT-

LOOK FOR MORE LOWER EARNINGS REPORTS BEFORE THE
PRIME RATE DECREASE TAKES EFFECT IN HELPING BUSI-
NESS—

A voice is amplified over the p.a. system: "Has anyone got the pink sheets?"

The automated board covers one entire long wall and keeps tabs on 171 leading stocks. There are seven assorted sets of averages, indices, and summaries. There are statistics for twelve commodity futures off in one area, including the prices of pork bellies for the months of May and July and the prices of sugar for July and September. Every time any of the numbers on any of these indices changes, there is a pronounced, clicking noise. Meanwhile, there are three separate teletype machines constantly chattering, any number of typewriters at work, and over thirty telephones.

But an old-timer can sit there slumped in his seat, his legs crossed, his cigar billowing, eyes flitting, relaxed but nevertheless the hunter, every click on that board, every fractional number a part of a vast complex of interlocking relationships stored in his mind, thousands of histories, phenomena, principles, studies, rules, exceptions, instances, mistakes, successes and failures that he has lived with, dreamed about and suffered under for years and years, all persuading his thoughts, his fear of being wrong, his anticipated joy of being right.

Nonchalantly, he listens to his murmuring neighbor:

"I don't know. I'm beginning to think if it does break eight hundred it won't be by very much. I'll tell you one thing, though. LTV has just about bottomed out."

They sit there—the investors, the traders and the

Boardroom Bums, all immersed in the clicks, the clacks, the clatterings, the bells, the buzz and hum of voices, the rings, the chings and the smoke, the nervousness, the hope, the bad luck, the greed and the agony. A little old lady comes wandering in wearing a crumpled house dress and an old plastic purse dangling from its strap. She decides to buy ten shares of AAC at 13½ because those are her daughter's initials. And from somewhere a loud, pedantic voice is droning on and on, explaining over and over again the logic behind his decision to buy into a power and light company in Idaho. The fish are biting extra early this year in the lakes. That means an extra cold winter. That means the utilities should make extra profits.

The voice is on the p.a. system again: "Has anyone got the pink sheets?"

It is 12:35. The tape is sluggish, moving in short, erratic spurts, the price changes very small and inconclusive. The volume is slight. The Dow-Jones average was plus 1.12 at the end of the first hour, but now it is plus .57 cents. There are very few large blocks being traded. It is the lunch hour on Wall Street. In the boardroom most of the seats are empty.

Two little old ladies make a quarter bet on whether the Dow-Jones will close on the plus side or the minus side. One of them changes account executives once a month and moves to a different brokerage house once a season. She insists on bringing her poodle into the boardroom. She places open orders to buy or sell at impossible prices above or below the market and then cancels abruptly if the price moves anywhere near an actual execution. Meanwhile, she insists on reference works, charts, research information and personal opinions. But her friend with the varicose veins and the flamingo shorts is a local pioneer, her family in tight control of at least two railroads.

If you go over to the Quotron machine and punch out the lettered keys that spell out the symbol of your stock and activate another button for the data desired, a series of numbers will be flashed on a miniature screen. You can learn the quoted bid-and-ask prices, the latest sale, the day's volume and any amount of related figures. Do you want yesterday's close for Big Steel? The price/earnings ratio of Ma Bell? The latest dividend paid by Bessie? The date of Girl's last split?

But if you punch out the letters GOD there is a brief computerized pause and then a zero appears in the upper right corner. You get the same answer for YES and NUT, for CAT and DOG.

The boardroom is full now. The phones are ringing. The teletype is chattering. The bald heads and the gray heads are all aimed up at the same angle. The cigar smoke is hanging in a low cumulus pall. One old man is asleep, his head slumped forward. The tape has been moving very rapidly. It stops. There is a hesitation and then a row of dots.

. . . . .MARKET CLOSED. . . . .

✳   ✳   ✳

The sixth leading cause of accidental death in the United States is choking to death on a piece of meat. It is called a "café coronary" and ranks ahead of gun accidents, plane crashes and electrocution and is only slightly behind drowning. Most of the victims are drunk. Most of these are elderly.

✳   ✳   ✳

He was eighty-two. He backed up in the supermarket parking lot and smashed into three other cars. When he moved forward the accelerator stuck. The car went out of control and crashed into nine more cars. The damage exceeded $10,000. He was charged with reckless driving.

✳   ✳   ✳

They were four old women from Canada. They dawdled over the drawbridge, unaware that it was opening. The rear tires caught over the edge and the car was hoisted high up in the air. The women were trapped for an hour and a half. The fire department arrived, raising extension ladders, securing the car with chains and helping them climb down.

21 Mr. Nitsch lives in Sunland Gardens, a rural development on the western edge of Fort Pierce. He came here in 1955, one of the first to buy a retirement home. Since then, very little has happened. The area is full of scrub pine and palmettos. Only a fraction of the lots have houses. Mr. Nitsch lives isolated at the dead end of one of the narrow streets beside a broad canal. His house is small, cheap, nestled in the second-growth forest that has sprung up in the tracks of the long-departed bulldozers.

On a wall of the living room is one of his amateurish paintings, a large woodland scene. Above it is a legend in large Greek letters that translates as "A thing of beauty is a joy forever."

The painting is fitted on rollers and has a supporting leg at the lower corner of the frame. When he pulls it out a diorama is revealed, an illuminated domed arch about four feet in diameter built into the wall. The scene is a

Japanese garden. Mt. Fuji is painted on a backdrop. In the foreground is a miniature pagoda, a bench, an arched footbridge, a mirror brook, and trees that are made of small pine cones dipped in green paint. Closer yet, still other trees are twigs from real pines. Above the arch is a legend written in clumsy, self-conscious ideograph characters that he copied out of a Japanese-English dictionary. It means "Let us sit down here and rest."

Propped up on the very edge of the scene is a small card typed with these words: "On the slopes of this sacred mountain the wreckage of a Boeing 707 was strewn with the bodies of all 124 aboard (34 Americans) and a newly wedded couple. March 5, 1966. It was a Bristol jet liner."

The back of the domed Japanese sky extends through the wall of the adjacent bedroom. On the convex side he had made a map of one fourth of the globe, choosing the quarter "that is in most of the trouble all the time." It extends from the pole to the equator, including all of Asia and most of Europe. On the wall above is another semicircular inscription in two-inch letters: "God has made of one blood all nations of men to dwell on the earth."

Mr. Nitsch says this is from the Bible, and it was meant to offset "that crazy prejudice they had down here when I first came. Against blacks. But now it's different. They're getting smart. And we're getting what we deserve."

Mr. Nitsch is tall. His hair is white but still quite thick. He wears a narrow gray mustache. He is dressed in a clean short-sleeve shirt with a striped necktie and a clasp, rumpled slacks and old bedroom slippers. His voice is a little high-pitched but still firm. He is nearly eighty-four years old.

He went to work when he was thirteen, getting three dollars a week at Bausch and Lomb in Rochester, New York. That was in 1903. He worked in the administration of several departments and then quit, calling it an old-fashioned firm. For the next fifteen years he did only odd jobs. He painted houses and gave art lessons, learned electronics by teaching himself. His wife died in 1940 after an operation to remove a stone in her pancreas. He went to work for Kodak in 1942 as a painter and decorator. In 1955, when he was sixty-five, he retired and came to Florida. He paid cash for his house and has no debts.

He has two sons. One is a teacher, the other a superintendent for DuPont. He doesn't get many letters, and a couple of years ago one of them finally came to visit, bringing along his ten-year-old grandson, whom he had never seen.

Parked across the street is a 1953 Ford with 40,000 miles on it. Mr. Nitsch has had cataract operations on both eyes, and his driver's license has been taken away. He has no peripheral vision, hasn't done any painting in two years, and has had several bad falls. Friends take him shopping regularly.

In his workshop the walls are hung with shelves and boxes of old and rusting tools of several different trades. A door that he built into one wall leads to another room he added himself. It is his art gallery, the walls covered with framed paintings, a rack of suspended masonite panels supporting oils done on canvas boards. Over the door is an inscription: "A Daybreak in Eden."

At the far end of the windowless, hot and stifling room

is another diorama, this one six feet wide, extending from a waist-high stage up to the ceiling. It is a replica of the Garden of Eden filled with plastic flowers, a cardboard Adam and Eve standing on a rock and holding hands and staring at the background sky. Their buttocks are naked and exposed in fine detail. The inscription: "The Heavens declare the glory of God and the firmament sheweth his handiwork."

Mr. Nitsch turns off the lights and throws switches. Several spotlights go on, but they are the wrong ones. Darkness again. And then the stars are shining in the dome of the Garden. The dawn begins at the lower edge. Lights on. Switches. Mr. Nitsch gets a shock as he fumbles with his salt-water rheostat, a Rube Goldberg contraption of plywood wheels and string pulleys, a jar of salt water, a conductor slowly lowered into the jar until it touches another pole on the bottom. At that point the current reaches its maximum 110 volts, and the sun is shining brightly over Eden. Then the old clockwork gears and the electric motor and the pulleys slowly retrieve the traveling pole. The water boils with the heat. The current weakens. The day slowly dims into twilight.

The stars are tiny bulbs imported from Japan. There are thirty-four in his universe, a dozen constellations of various circuits arranged in series. Changing a burned-out star requires long and patient testing.

He smiles at his pun when he refers to life being just another "niche." He struggles with the timers and the electronic paraphernalia that is supposed to synchronize the taped sound effects and the narration with the salt-water rheostat cycle of daylight. Behind a painting beneath the diorama is a hidden speaker. Back in the living room he plays around with the tape recorder. Suddenly Nitsch's voice comes through in a high female falsetto:

"Adam? Will you always love me?"

And then Nitsch as a masculine baritone:

"How can I help it?"

There is the sharp, sucking sound of a wet kiss. There is piano music. "The World Is Waiting for the Sunrise."

Mr. Nitsch stops the tape, runs it forward, runs it back, looking for interesting sections. Snatches of Johann Strauss's "Thunder and Lightning Polka" are interspersed with a home-made recording of real thunder plus a crackle of artificial lightning created in Mr. Nitsch's workshop.

Falsetto:

"I am afraid."

Baritone:

"Don't be afraid, little girl."

Snatches of Handel's "Largo." An album jacket hangs by a string from a lighting fixture on the wall. It is Anita Bryant's "Abide with Me."

Baritone:

". . . and the stars reappear . . . now listen to the confidence as expressed by the birds . . ."

Twittering of birds. Plastic flowers in vases. A violin on the living-room floor. Books. Typewriter. On the ceiling, a six-foot round geometric floral pattern of vaguely Hindu inspiration. A color print of the Nixon family taped to the side of the TV. Unidentifiable gadgets. Miniature bronze reproductions of "The Thinker" as bookends. A color chart of the chemical elements fastened to the workshop door. A small mirror fitted on an adjustable bracket in the frame of the window so you can see who is approaching the front door.

Falsetto:

"Adam? Isn't this marvelous?"

Baritone:

"Yes. It is, my darling."

Eve begins to sing with Marian Anderson's voice. There are two dozen ballpoint pens by the phone stuck through screw-eyes fastened to the edge of the table. As Mr. Nitsch pushes the buttons, stops, rewinds and plays back, he begins to sing out loud, his voice quavering, absent-minded, joyful:

". . . as the skies begin to fall . . ."

Another day in the Garden of Eden comes to a close with the sounds of owls and nightingales. Mr. Nitsch's voice is soothing and reassuring:

". . . as the timid stars venture out again . . . as a perfect day is ended . . . as we behold the mighty works of God's creation . . ."

The backyard is all leaves and pine needles, a ficus tree devouring all available sunlight, a night-blooming cereus growing up the trunk of an Australian pine in a climb of desperation. There is a windmill. There is a steel pole with a toy monkey on top. It is supposed to come down in spiraling circles, but it doesn't work anymore. There is a mill and a turning float in a miniature canal. There is a speaker hidden in a toy castle buried in the overgrown palmetto bush. Some of the goldfish are still alive. Mr. Nitsch points out the bridge that spans the canal. A tiny sign says ONE WAY, but the toy cars are nevertheless pointed in every direction in such a snarl that a toy doll "hippie" leaps over the bridge railing in despair.

Only a few pigeons are left in the coop. The rest have been stolen by neighborhood black boys who regularly climb the low fence to tear things up and steal whatever is lying around. He lost his pruning saw just a few days ago. In the shadows stands an Indian statue holding a vertical spear. Mr. Nitsch calls it his sentry.

He has rigged an involved toy for the squirrels, putting peanuts on the ends of flexible wires next to a rotating drum. It amuses him to watch their frenzied acrobatics every morning. Over a picnic pavilion in the corner is a sign: SUN HAVEN. It is his name for the house. A telephone extension is in a box on a tree. He has two outside bells in the front and back yards.

Plastic hoses, pipes and wires are strewn on the ground. There is a white disk with an indicator and black markings. Mr. Nitsch kneels down and tries to adjust it. There is a fountain in the little canal that is supposed to squirt up and hold a red ping-pong ball in perfect balance. But it isn't working. Nor can he start the mechanical moth that was designed to fly in fluttering circles from the end of a supple wire.

The screened-in Florida room is jammed with old furniture, a rubber snake entwined among the chain of brass chimes hanging on the screen door. More paintings and more plastic flowers, a Mexican-peasant-and-burro scene within a painted arch on the wall that he pretends is a window. There are some tropical fish, some real African violets, a solid oak desk that he bought in Rochester for $18 in 1909 when he was nineteen years old. He explains how he converted the room from the original carport, doing all the work himself, laying the asphalt tiles on the floor and closing in the walls.

Mr. Nitsch says he maintains a variety of interests to

keep from getting lonely. "Like this friend of mine. He just sits on his hands. Waiting for the end. And some others. It's all doom and gloom."

Back in the living room he fiddles with the cuckoo clock in the corner. It works almost immediately.

* * *

He was eighty-two. He was crossing an intersection on his tricy-
cle with the green light. The light changed. A truck started up,
dragging him 100 feet and cutting off most of his head.

* * *

22 At Baptist Village in Pompano Beach, Mrs. Miller, a spry woman in her early sixties, is pushing her husband around in a wheelchair. He has already had his hair cut and is being wheeled from room to room behind the barber, his wife holding the money for several different patients, all collected from visiting relatives. She is wearing a pastel-blue pants suit. Her hair is blue-gray and freshly set. She is very talkative, quick and decisive.

The Millers came from Indianapolis, where he was a monument cutter. She set the letters and he operated the sandblasting machine. "Of course, he's paying for it now. He has sand in his lungs." Mrs. Miller speaks behind his back very loudly. Her husband never moves, slumped in the chair under a lap robe. His hair is very thin, his skin dry, his ear lobes long and shiny, resembling old wax. His face never changes its empty, stiffened expression. Sometimes he raises his eyes for a long moment. And then without recognition, without reason, without expression, his eyes drop and look at nothing.

The woman goes on talking. They had always taken their vacations in Florida. Her husband started ailing in 1957. But since bronze markers had largely replaced tombstones, they didn't manage to sell their business until 1960. They came to Florida and bought a house in 1964. "But now he's failing so rapidly." Her voice is very loud. Mr. Miller doesn't move. His eyes never blink.

Mrs. Miller is now selling the house and moving to an apartment at Baptist Village. She has bought a $10,000 investment bond from them, drawing 9 percent interest. If anything happens to her, she will be taken care of. She doesn't mention the possibility of her husband sharing the apartment with her.

Baptist Village is a church-city of the retired with apartments and private cottages. The grounds are professionally landscaped. Everything is very new. For an initial lump sum paid to the church and then a monthly service fee, you will be taken care of, provided with housing and food, for the rest of your life. The nursing home annex has wall-to-wall carpeting everywhere. All is contemporary, decorated and air-conditioned, the rooms arranged like those of a hospital, but the colors and the furniture like those of a modern hotel. But when you pass by the open doors you can see the ancient bodies inside, curled up on the beds without moving, lying in fetal positions, dozing upright in their chairs, thin, ill, white-haired, silent.

The aides and the nurses come and go. One of them is trying to calm an old man so the barber can do his hair. But he keeps yelling out in a booming voice: "Where's

it at now? Son of a bitch? What are you doing to her?
WHERE'S IT AT NOW?"

There are giggles—the barber and the nurse maintain-
ing their cool, amused by the deranged senilities they are
trying to control. Yet they are embarrassed, overwhelmed by the magic and the totem of the very old, the
very ill and the insane.

Across the hallway and down a few rooms, another
voice calls out, faltering, very frightened.

"Sarah? Sarah?"

Mrs. Miller continues to explain how everything is
taken care of and prearranged if anything should happen
to her. Her husband sits in the wheelchair without moving. And then he raises his head and looks up. There is
no expression, no shift, no mood, only the dim glow of
two bluish indicator lamps burning very faintly.

23 There are seven of them, all operated by the Florida Department of Commerce. There is one on U.S. 27 near the town of Havana, another on U.S. 19 just north of Monticello. There is another near Campbellton on U.S. 231 and one west of Pensacola on U.S. 90. There is also a Marine Welcome Station at Fernandina Beach where yachts navigating the Intracoastal Waterway can receive the state's official hospitality.

And then there is the first welcome station ever built anywhere in the country. You enter Florida on U.S. 17 just above Yulee. Crossing the St. Mary's River over a narrow, steel girder bridge at 35 mph, you are jerked by the bumps and the rattling gratings. The water is black from the primeval organic matter decaying in the swamps. There are water hyacinths and lilies and dead stumps burned black. There is a line of palms and then a wayside park.

There is another station at Boulogne where the banks of the St. Mary's are steep, the trees tall and attractive. FLORIDA is spelled out against a screening wall embellished with palms and magnolias. The sign is at the end of the concrete bridge. It is illuminated at night. The road is a divided highway, a junction of U.S. 1, U.S. 23, and U.S. 301.

Muzak. Begonias and philodendrons. Posters on the walls, each of a different scene with the slogan "One of 12 great regions in Florida." Water skiing. A kid on the beach with a sand bucket. Sailing boats. A couple walking in the surf. A rocket being launched. Picking oranges from horseback. Surfboarding. Airboats. Scuba diving. Yachting. Kids poling a raft. Spanish costumes at St. Augustine.

In the busy season they give away 100 gallons of free orange juice a day. Today they gave away thirteen. There are free folders about zoos, race tracks, hotels, natural springs, wild animal farms, and museums. Busch Gardens. Kennedy Space Center. Aquatarium. Fountain of Youth. There is a mounted bass attached to a polished natural cypress knee.

The blue background of the big sign outside has become powdered by the rays of the sun. Innumerable names have been written in the dust by rubbing fingers.

The receptionists can rattle off the exact mileage to any city in Florida. All of them love people and never get bored with saying the same things over and over. May is the slowest month. The summer is the busiest, the season of the family vacationers.

A fat man in a camper truck from New Jersey had a trailer in Riviera Beach. He spent half his time in

Florida. He would like to stay all year, but his wife
wanted to visit their grandchildren. He had a heart condition. He had been all over the United States and also
overseas.

"Florida can't be beat."

An old couple got out of a car with North Carolina
tags. He stood there shaking, his eyes moving left and
right to see who was watching. Softly he muttered to his
wife, "I'm gonna need a little help."

Coming around from the driver's side, she guided him
to the sidewalk. With a quick, shuffling gait he made it
to the entrance. Then he stopped. There was a long
hesitation before he could get his right leg to move again.
It was the same thing coming back. He walked right
along and then stopped as though a wire had been cut,
as though he had suddenly forgotten how to walk. His
wife talked in his ear, rocking him back and forth by the
elbow, like a wooden soldier whose spring had become
stuck.

Sedans. Coupes. Station wagons. Impala. Pinto.
Chrysler. Massachusetts. Virginia. New York. Toyota.
Volkswagen. Maine.

You drive south on I-75 just above Jennings. There are
a few plowed fields scattered among the scrub pine
woods. There are a few billboards. The sky is clear. A
carful of tourists pulls over and stops. They are wearing
Bermuda shorts and bathing suits. They take pictures of
one another in front of a blue sign with an orange fac-
simile of the map. The sign says WELCOME TO FLORIDA—
THE SUNSHINE STATE. A smaller sign nearby says ARRIVE
ALIVE.

Another 1.6 miles. OFFICIAL FLORIDA WELCOME STATION.

Landscaped shrubs. Spanish bayonets. Holly bushes. Phone booths. Diagonal parking. Forty-two cars and five assorted campers, trucks and trailers. Kids' playground. Beds of gravel. Palms. Arbor vitae. A hose, faucet and sign: SELF-SERVICE WINDSHIELD WASHING. CARS ONLY. Motors stop and start. Cars come in and pull out. The traffic moves by on the throughway doing eighty. Drone. Swish. Whistle. "No pets allowed." Trash bins. An old woman with a white poodle on a leash is talking to herself. A pole with the American and Florida flags.

Mr. and Mrs. James Tait drove up in a silver-gray Mercury. Love bugs were encrusted on the windshield and on the front grill and headlights. He had a shock of gray hair and wore a yellow sport shirt and mustard-brown pants and black shoes. She was big-bosomed and wore a pink dress. Her hair was frizzled and gray. The back seat was filled with clothes. There was a red purse on the front seat, a road map stuck under the handles. There was a hairbrush, snapshots, a compass on the dashboard, a fan on the back shelf, a neck-rest pillow. He had just retired and bought a house in South Venice, where he had many friends. He wanted to get away from the snow and the cold in Michigan. Florida had fulfilled his expectations thus far, but he had only retired the first of the year and was just moving in.

"I don't know what I'm going to do until I get there. Work on the house first for a little while. Make some changes. I don't know. Just carry on, I guess. Just the way we have been. I'll wait till I get there."

Bicycles lashed on top of a station wagon. Car hoods raised. People eating at the picnic tables. Kids playing. Groups of people pass one another walking to and from their cars. Jeans. Shorts. Sunglasses. A woman balances four small paper cups of orange juice in her hands. It is air-conditioned inside. The receptionists are dressed in Kelly-green double-breasted jackets and dark-blue slacks and white shoes. Information. Rest rooms. The crowd churns in and out.

"Would you like some juice?"

"How many are in your party?"

"Welcome to Florida."

"Where are you from?"

"Welcome to Florida."

"Thank you and have a nice trip."

"How many are in your party?"

"Would you like some juice?"

A stack of papers: *Mobile Home Owners Guide.* A rack of literature. Folders. Illuminated transparencies of Daytona Beach, Sunken Gardens, White Springs, the sport-fishing fleet at Pompano Beach. Phone booth. A fat man with sunglasses confused by the *Xerox Microfilm Reader,* which gives information on hotel rates and vacancies and seasonal dates.

"What state are you from?"

"Where is your destination?"

"Welcome to Florida."

Multicolored croton bush in a pot. Water fountain. Sweaters. Tee shirts. Platform shoes. Cigarettes. Hair curlers. "Please limit orange juice to one cup per person." Moving color slides of the Stephen Foster Memorial on the Swanee River. "Free Florida room reservations. Pick up direct phone to reservations operator." Free magazines: *Sun Fun Country* and *Space Coast.* Ponytails. Cutoffs. Sandals. Pale skin. Varicose veins. Denim. Purple. Pink. Baseball caps.

I-75 is the busiest welcome station in the state. Built on

five acres, it was obsolete in less than a year. They have already enlarged the building and added the rest rooms outside. In addition to the eleven receptionists, two men work on the grounds. There is a full-time maid, a part-time maid, and a maintenance man.

On the record day 14,000 people entered between 8:00 A.M. and 5:00 P.M.—twenty-six people per minute. People were lined up to get in. All 124 parking spaces were filled and cars backed up out into the traffic until the Highway Patrol had to be called. They gave away 350 gallons of orange juice.

Ann Hiers is the supervisor, a veteran of eighteen and a half years. She has been marking off maps over the counter so long that when she goes on a trip herself she has to hold the map upside down. She thinks people are funny. They ask weird questions, but they return the friendliness they are offered. They are on vacation. They are happy. She has often heard the comments "We've never been to Florida before. But we're never going home. As soon as we crossed the line, we loved it."

Sneakers. Bare feet. Chartreuse pants. A patio outside the glass doors and the roaring air conditioners. Purses. A sheath knife. Beard. Cigars. Paper cups. Neckties. Pipes. Bulletin board with pictures, calendars, weather and fishing reports.

H. E. Wehr would be seventy on his next birthday. He spoke clearly and well. He was well dressed, just a little bent by his age. He drove a chartreuse Cadillac with a white top. He had lived at Boynton Beach with his wife for five years. But they were leaving. Their apartment was for sale, and they had bought a house back where they came from in Tennessee. They weren't disappointed in Florida, really. It had been fabulous. But it was just getting too damned crowded. His wife said the sewer and water conditions were terrible. There were 8,000 people in Boynton Beach when they arrived. In five years it had become 25,000 and everybody said it would be 75,000 in three more years.

Mr. and Mrs. Trombley were coming down to visit and to look around. He had come down once when he was sixty-five, and now that he was seventy-five he was going to look again. He was a sales engineer and a manufacturer's representative. He had already been retired once but went back to work. They would start at West Palm Beach and work their way south. They liked everything about Florida. She liked the sun. They both liked to swim and loved the ocean. He intended to play golf. They had moved from Cincinnati to Detroit and to New England and Philadelphia and back again.

"We're in Ohio. And what is there in Ohio?"

They might not live here all year round, but the summers were just as hot up north. It was very humid in Cincinnati. Everybody had sinus trouble. They drove a Cadillac. He wore a wide mod belt and belled slacks. She wore a neat striped dress.

Buick. Fury. Mercury. Michigan. Illinois. Ohio. Park and use the john. Get some o.j. and a free map. Leave. Datsun. Windstream. Motorcyclists with bedrolls. Young marrieds. The sun is hot. The breeze is cool. A spry man in plaid slacks says he already lives in Florida. Yes. He is satisfied.

Another couple were coming down for a week to look over some property. They might move down but weren't sure. He had not retired yet. They wanted to look at some lots at Lehigh Acres. They weren't too sure where that was. Somewhere on the west coast near Fort Myers, they thought.

No. He would not be happy in Florida. Didn't know anybody here. Besides. It wasn't like Georgia.

Windshield covered with love bugs. Boat trailer. U-Haul. EZ Haul. Big Diesel semi roaring in and out. Mustang. SS 396. Lincoln Continental. Turning signals flash. Zoom. Roar. Squeal. Chevy Van 30. Car top carriers. Baby cribs. Phone booth.

"Didi? We've just crossed the line into Florida. How is everything? Where's Jim? Oh, yeah. It's hot here."

Pickup truck with a tarp. Campers. Two women taking pictures. Tattoos. Wrinkles. Bermudas. Bells. Tote bags.

"What is this for? You gonna put us in touch with real-estate people?"

Bifocals. Honda attached to the rear bumper of a Ford Galaxie. Tee shirts: "Keep on truckin." Panty hose. No bra. Four white-haired ladies, one putting her gum into a trash basket. Girl with Canadian crutches and a brace on one leg.

The traffic swishes and roars on I-75.

John E. Hughes lived in Sunrise, next to Fort Lauderdale. He had been visiting his wife's family and his grandchildren in Georgia and Kentucky and was now going home. He was sixty-seven and had been retired six and a half years. He was tall, with a slumped belly and a gaunt face. He wore a sport-fishing cap with crossed signal flags and spoke very slowly.

"We're enjoyin' ourse'f. Goin' along with the flow. It's real nice down here. Yeah. It's real good. We watch

television. Cut the grass. Work in the yard. Take care of
our—you know. Go to the doctor and the grocery store.
She goes to church. Belongs to her own club. I'm really
happy. I worked for General Motors for thirty-six years.
I got a good pension. I got no . . . uh . . . really no
problems. Desperation problems. You know what I
mean."

Dr. Ellis D. Tooker just retired at fifty-seven. It was
fun so far, but he might have guilt feelings about not
using his skills, not producing, not using his experience
to solve some of the current social problems. He took his
Ph.D in psychology at Harvard. He had been assistant
superintendent of schools in Hartford, Connecticut.
They had a new home in Sebring but were dubious
about Florida. It might be too crowded. They expected
to stay six months of the year and do a lot of traveling.
They drove a Globestar camper with a 5 x 12 U-Haul
trailer covered with a tarpaulin and tied ropes. Clothes
and furniture and a large black dog were visible through
the windows. They had stickers on the back from Key
West Boyd's Campground and South Padre Island,
Texas, and Mexico and Disneyland Area KOA and
Longkey. He had been stationed in Florida during
World War II, and their oldest son had been born in
Jacksonville. He liked to fish and to hunt. He might do
a little writing.

House car from Indiana. A white Dodge parks next to
a sign—RESERVED FOR HANDICAPPED—and blocks the
wheelchair ramp. A new private bus with a radiotele-
phone number on the rear window. Sign by the door:
CHARLES AND LOIS VAN HORN. MIDDLETOWN, OHIO. A kid falls
and screeches. Four old ladies from Illinois. An old man

from Colorado with a silver and turquoise belt. Two hippies from Ontario. Three barefoot, bare-chested guys with gold rings in their ears. Butts litter the grass. Paper cups roll in the wind. The sky is clear. It is hot. The traffic swishes to the north. It roars to the south.

"In other words, I stay right on I-75."

"To the Florida Turnpike. Understand?"

"Fine. Thank you."

"I hope you enjoy your new home."

"Thank you. I do too."

"Sir? I've been looking for someone just like you who is moving to Florida. Do you have a moment?"

"Well, I'm really . . . I'm tired and I don't want to talk at this time. Believe me, I've been on the road since seven o'clock this morning. No. Some other time maybe."

"I was just interested in getting your views on Florida and what you expected from—"

"I don't know. I expect it to be a very, very . . . uh . . . relaxing life."

"You've been down here before, haven't you?"

"I've been down on visits, but I've never been here . . . to live. But I've decided now that I'm gonna live. So we're gonna . . . we're gonna take a little . . . uh . . . time down here and see whether we like it or not. But I'm sure it'll be all right."

He handed a cup of orange juice to his wife, who did not get out of the car. He started the motor, hesitated briefly at the end of the driveway, and roared out into the traffic.

ABOUT THE AUTHOR

Age 4: Depression. Father travelling sign painter and carnival concessionaire. Hitchhiked with mother and sister. Cold. Tired. Begged food in restaurants. Slept at Salvation Army.

Age 11: Many schools: Carolinas, Virginia, Florida, Philadelphia, New York.

Age 13: Began work. Dishwasher and farmhand.

Age 14: Shipyard. Machinist's helper. Night shift.

Age 15: Quit school. Hitchhiker. Freight trains. Odd jobs.

Age 16: Booted out of army after release from stockade.

Age 17: Merchant seaman.

Age 18: Europe and India. Beachcomber. Black market. Opium. Counterfeit dollars. Riviera jail. One year. Escaped. Deserted Norwegian ship. Returned to U.S.

Age 19: Safecracker. Opened 26.

Age 20: Caught. Two years at hard labor. Three years suspended. Began writing.

Age 22: Released. Returned to sea. Continued writing.

Age 29: Third Mate.

Age 31: Living in Brooklyn cellar. Leg smashed. Nearly amputated. Crutches for two years. Motorcycle.

Age 33: Married: Christine. Former nurse.

Age 36: First published. *Cool Hand Luke*. Novel based on chain gang experience.

Age 39: Nominated. Academy Award. Screenplay.

Age 40: Three sons: Hawser, Anker, Rudder. Journalist: Esquire, Playboy, Miami Herald and others.

Age 43: Second novel. *Pier Head Jump.* Based on sea experience.

Age 45: Living in Florida. Broke. Still writing.